faith
MATTERS
FOR YOUNG ADULTS

W9-DFK-669

practicing the faith

Abingdon Press / Nashville

FAITH MATTERS FOR YOUNG ADULTS
PRACTICING THE FAITH

ISBN 0-687-49370-6

MANUFACTURED IN THE UNITED STATES OF AMERICA

06 07 08 09 10 11 12 13 14 15—10 9 8 7 6 5 4 3 2 1

Contents

Welcome to Faith Matters for Young Adults

Faith does matter! All adults—whether young, middle-aged, or older—yearn to believe in something. The psalmist wrote:

"As a deer longs for flowing streams, so my soul longs for you, O God." (Psalm 42:1)

This resource begins with the basic assumption that human beings seek to ground their lives in something or someone beyond themselves. As Christians, we further believe that who or what is at the center of a person's life matters greatly.

Faith mattered to biblical people. Throughout the Bible, persons faced decisions concerning in what or in whom they should stake their lives and their souls. **Joshua** called the Israelites to choose whom they would serve—the gods of the Egyptians and the Amorites or the God who had led them out of slavery. **Elijah** forced the people of Israel to decide whether they would permit Baal or the Lord to shape their lives and destinies. **The prophets** called the people to change their lives, to move away from immorality, to choose instead lives of justice and righteousness that were worthy of the worship of the one true God. **Jesus** warned people that they could not serve two masters. He counseled that faith in God was better than shaping one's life around money or personal prestige. Faith continues to matter. Faith dictates the shape one's living takes.

If we think of the word *matters* as a verb rather than as a noun, we can say that faith takes substantial shape as we make choices and act day by day. Faith involves both belief and practice, in other words. Because we believe that God is just and merciful, we choose to be just and merciful. We practice serving others because we believe God in Christ calls us to serve others. Faith matters—takes shape—as we act upon what we believe.

You might also think about *faith matters* as referring to the actual topics of the sessions. What are the "matters" of faith? In three study books we offer sessions that will help view the Christian faith through three different lenses. Sessions in **Discovering the Faith** will help you learn more about matters related to the basic beliefs of Christian faith. Sessions in **PRACTICING THE FAITH** will help you engage matters of faith through worship and participation in the ministries of a church, through the practice of Christian disciplines, and through the search for answers to challenging questions about God. Sessions in *Living the Faith* will help you explore what it means to live as a Christian and connect matters of faith to matters of everyday life.

Using the Books in Faith Matters for Young Adults

The titles of each of the sessions in the Faith Matters for Young Adults books are stated as questions. Adults of all ages have questions about faith and belief. Few expect to be satisfied with simple answers; however, it is important to engage matters of faith and belief by being willing to engage the questions. Such engagement, with God's presence and guidance, inevitably leads to faith development. Faith Matters for Young Adults seeks to help you engage the questions, discern what is at stake for your faith, and move you toward an understanding that will guide you as you grow in love of God and neighbor.

At the beginning of each book you will find

♦ suggestions for starting a Faith Matters for Young Adults group
♦ suggestions for different ways to use the book
♦ suggestions for leading a group

In each of the sessions you will find

♦ a focus statement that illuminates the content of the session;
♦ gathering and closing worship experiences related to the focus of each session;
♦ space to write reflections or insights evoked by topics in the main content;
♦ concise, easy-to-use leader/learner helps near the main text to which they refer;
♦ main content rich with illustrations from contemporary life and reliable information about the Scriptures in each session.

The three small-group study books in Faith Matters for Young Adults are designed for versatility of use in a variety of settings.

Small groups on Sunday morning (45 to 60 minutes). Sunday morning groups generally last 45 to 60 minutes. If your group would like to go into greater depth, you can divide the sessions and do the study for longer than seven weeks.

Weekday or weeknight groups (60 to 90 minutes). We recommend 90-minute sessions for a weekday or weeknight study. Participants should prepare ahead by reading the content of the session and choosing one activity for deeper reflection and study.

A weekend retreat. For a weekend retreat, distribute the books at least two weeks in advance. Locate and provide additional media resources and reference materials, such as hymnbooks, Bibles, Bible dictionaries and commentaries, and other books. If possible, have a computer with Internet capabilities on site. Ask participants to read their study books before the retreat. Begin on Friday with an evening meal or refreshments followed by gathering time and worship. Create a schedule that will allow you to cover the 13 sessions during the weekend.

Individual devotion and reflection. While the books are designed for small-group study, they can also be beneficial for individual devotion and reflection. Read the Scriptures, then read the main content of the sessions. Adapt the questions in the leader/learner boxes to help you reflect upon the issues related to the biblical theme.

Organizing a Faith Matters for Young Adults Group

Faith Matters for Young Adults is an excellent small-group study for young adults who seek to know more about the faith, about church, and about living one's faith in daily life. Some of these young adults may not be a part of a faith community, and yet they are seekers on a profound spiritual journey. They may be new Christians or new members who want to know more about Christian faith or who want to make new friends in a faith community. Or they may be people who have been in church a long time but who feel a need for spiritual renewal. This study invites all these young adults to engage more deeply with issues of faith and with the Bible in order to find meaning and hope.

Starting a Faith Matters for Young Adults study group is an effective way to involve young adults in the life of your local church. Follow the steps below to help you get started.

♦ Read through the Faith Matters for Young Adults study book. Think about the questions and the focus for each of the sessions. Prepare to respond to questions that someone may ask about the study.

♦ Decide on a location and time for your Faith Matters for Young Adults group.

♦ Develop a list of potential participants. An ideal size for a small group is 7 to 12 people. Your list should have about twice your target number (14 to 24 people). Ask your local church to purchase a copy of the study book for each of the persons on your list.

♦ Identify someone who is willing to go with you to visit the persons on your list. Make it your goal to become acquainted with each person you visit. Tell those you visit about Faith Matters for Young Adults. Give them a copy of the study book. Even if they choose not to attend the small group at this time, they will have an opportunity to study the book on their own. Tell each person the initial meeting time and location and how many weeks the group will meet. Invite them to become a part of the group. Thank them for their time.

♦ Publicize the new Faith Matters for Young Adults study through as many channels as are available. Announce it during worship. Print notices in the church newsletter and bulletin and on the church Web site, if you have one. Use free public event notices in community newspapers. Create fliers for mailing and posting in public places.

♦ A few days before the session begins, give a friendly phone call or send a note to thank all the persons you visited for their consideration and interest. Remind them of the time and location of the first meeting.

For more detailed instructions about starting and maintaining a small group, read *How to Start and Sustain a Faith-Based Small Group*, by John D. Schroeder (Abingdon, 2003).

Leading a Faith Matters for Young Adults Group

A group may have one leader for all the sessions, or leadership may be rotated among the participants. Leaders do not need to be experts in Bible study because the role of the leader is to facilitate discussion rather than to teach a particular content. Both leader and learner use the same book and commit to read and prepare for the session each week. So what does the leader do?

A Leader Prepares for the Session

Pray. Ask for God's guidance as you prepare to lead the session.

Read the session and its Scriptures ahead of time. List questions or insights that occur during the reading. Make a list of any needed supplies.

Think about group participants. Who are they? What life issues or questions might they have about faith?

Prepare ahead. Gather any needed supplies, such as large sheets of paper, markers, paper and pencils, Bibles, hymnbooks, audiovisual equipment, masking tape, a Bible dictionary, Bible commentaries, a Bible atlas. Session 1 includes creating nametags and serving a simple meal. Gather supplies for making the nametags. Decide what kind of meal you would like to serve. Something like pizza or chili is easy to prepare and serve. If you are meeting in a classroom setting, arrange the chairs in a circle or around a table. Make sure everyone will have a place to sit.

Create a worship center. Find a small table. Cover it with an attractive cloth. Place a candle in a candleholder in the center. Place matches nearby to light the candle. Place a Bible or other items that relate to the session focus in the worship center.

Pray. Before the participants arrive, pray for each one. Ask for God's blessing on your session. Offer thanks to God for the opportunity to lead the session.

A Leader Creates a Welcoming Atmosphere

Hospitality is a spiritual discipline. A leader helps to create an environment that makes others feel welcome and that helps every participant experience the freedom to ask questions and to state opinions. Such an atmosphere is based upon mutual respect.

Greet participants as they arrive. Say their names. If the class is meeting for the first time, use nametags.

Listen. As group discussion unfolds, affirm the comments and ideas of participants. Avoid the temptation to dominate conversation or "correct" the ideas of other participants.

Affirm. Thank people for telling about what they think or feel. Acknowledge their contributions to discussion in positive ways, even if you disagree with their ideas.

A Leader Facilitates Discussion

Ask questions. Use the questions suggested in the leader/learner helps or other questions that occurred to you as you prepared for the session. Encourage others to ask questions.

Invite silent participants to contribute ideas. If someone in the group is quiet, you might say something like: "I'm interested in what you are thinking." If they seem hesitant or shy, do not pressure them to speak. Do communicate your interest. If one participant dominates conversation, remind the group that everyone's ideas are important. Again, invite those who are quiet to express their ideas.

Be willing to say, "I don't know." A leader is also a learner. You are not "teaching" a defined content to a group of "students." Instead, you are helping others and yourself to engage faith matters that emerge from discovering, practicing, and living Christian faith.

Faith Matters for Young Adults: Practicing the Faith

Session 1

What Does Practicing the Faith Mean?

Pamela Dilmore

FOCUS This session introduces the 13-week study, PRACTICING THE FAITH, a book in the series Faith Matters for Young Adults. It invites you to engage the challenging questions about life and God, to support and be supported by a church family, and to practice Christian disciplines that will help you grow in faith and become aware of God's presence and love in all of life.

– GATHERING –

Create a nametag. Write your name and one question you have about practicing the Christian faith on a small piece of construction paper. Use either masking tape or a straight pin to attach your nametag to your clothing. Find another person. Tell each other what you wrote on the nametag.

Share a meal, such as pizza or chili, with the group. As you eat, tell the larger group what you and your partner wrote on your nametags. On a sheet of poster paper or other large writing surface, list all the questions raised about practicing the Christian faith. Display the list throughout the remaining sessions. Save your nametag. You will use it during closing worship.

Sing together the hymn "Sanctuary," "Cry of My Heart," or another praise chorus or song about wanting to live and worship as a Christian. You can find the songs mentioned above in *The Faith We Sing* (Abingdon Press) or in other books of praise songs and hymns.

Pray together the Lord's Prayer.

Practicing Our Faith

What does it mean to "practice" our faith? Either we have faith or we don't, right? In one sense, you could say that a person believes or does not believe; but the reality of Christian faith is that it involves belief *and* action, both of which are God's grace-filled gifts through Jesus Christ. The Second Chapter of James unpacks the relationship between faith and works and articulates this understanding: "What good is it, my brothers and sisters, if you say you have faith but do not have works?" (verse 14). Our faith has a content. It calls for belief and action that demonstrate love of God and neighbor. God creates, loves, and sustains all creation. We see God's salvation and God's nature clearly in Jesus Christ, in his life, his ministry, his death, and his resurrection. God's life and salvation continue to empower us and sustain us through God's Holy Spirit as we seek to serve God and neighbor.

> How do you understand the connections between belief and action? Read James 2. How do you respond to the ideas about faith and works?

As we claim the rich, life-giving realities associated with the content of our faith, we also claim the invitation to live with courage and hope for today and for the future, no matter what happens. Believing in the content of our faith leads us to respond to God's call with our daily choices and actions. We make connections between what God has done and continues to do through Jesus Christ, connections that can make a difference in our lives and in the lives of those around us. Faith is not simple assent to a set of principles or to a doctrine. As God's gift of grace, it has the life-giving power to move us in directions that increase our desire to love and serve God and our neighbor.

Spiritual Growth

Acting out of our belief involves all of our lives. *Discovering the Faith* offers opportunities to explore the content of the Christian faith. *Living the Faith* explores what it means to live out the faith in down-to-earth ways in everyday life. This book, PRACTICING THE FAITH, explores opportunities to learn about and to engage in traditional Christian practices that will nurture our faith in all of life, in the good times and in the difficult times.

On the one hand, we recognize that becoming Christian does not mean that life will be without suffering. Challenging questions emerge from our experiences of and knowledge about loss, horror, terror, injustice, catastrophic disaster, or life-threatening circumstances of illness or war. On the other hand is our faith.

> What connections do you see between Christian spiritual growth and life situations that may cause suffering? How have you, or how has someone you know, experienced God's presence in good times? in difficult times? In what ways, if any, were church, prayer, Bible reading, or giving involved?

Christians seek viable ways to engage the challenging questions and to respond faithfully. The process of seeking God's way in Jesus Christ in all of life's circumstances is what Christian spiritual growth is all about. We grow spiritually when we engage our minds and hearts with Christian practices and disciplines through which we become more aware of God's love for all creation. We attend church. We worship God. We participate in the sacraments of Holy Communion and baptism. We read the Bible. We pray. We meet in small groups to study, to learn from one another, to nurture one another. We offer time, talents, and treasure to the ministries of our church. We find ways to serve others. We give our money to charity. Such practices contribute to our spiritual growth in Christian faith.

Practice, Practice, Practice!

PRACTICING THE FAITH intentionally uses the word *practice* with regard to Christian faith. For most of us, the word evokes the experience of repeating an activity or engaging in it frequently in order to learn something, to develop a skill, or to instill a habit. Used in this way, the word is a verb. Musicians must practice in order to learn how to play an instrument. Singers must sing to develop voice and range. Athletes must practice in order to develop skill and endurance in a sport. Writers must write, painters must paint, sculptors must sculpt. Teachers learn by teaching. Carpenters learn to build by building. Every skill, in some way, involves daily practice.

Practice also can be a noun as suggested in the doing of a profession that requires a certain expertise or knowledge, such as "the practice of law" or "the practice of medicine." Writing, painting, sculpting, teaching, and constructing are practices that require a specific knowledge.

Lance Armstrong overcame cancer and won Le Tour de France bicycle race seven times consecutively. Golfer Tiger Woods and tennis champions Serena and Venus Williams are known throughout the world for their athletic skills. The Dave Matthews Band developed their music by practicing and playing together and by touring college campuses year after year to share their music. All these people, and others like them in sports, music, and other professions, understand the value of practice.

Take a moment now and recall something you "practiced" when you were growing up. Write or make sketches about that "practice" in the space below:

What Christian "practice" has been meaningful to you? What practices do you think might be meaningful to you? Which ones might nurture your faith?

Living the Christian life from day to day involves particular "practices" that support us as we grow in our faith and hope in God. We have many opportunities to experience God's grace as we attend Sunday school and worship service, as we participate in the sacraments of Holy Communion and baptism or in other worship rituals, as we become participants of small groups that gather to study or explore a faith issue or topic, as we read the Bible, as we pray, and as we reach out to others through service. Such practices help us to become more aware of God's presence, power, and love. Through participation in such practices, we grow closer to God, both as individuals and as communities of faith.

Discipline

Another word closely associated with *practice* is the word *discipline*. Many people associate this word with punishment that is intended to teach a lesson to someone, as when a parent "disciplines" a child. The word actually means far more than "punishment." *The Webster's New World Dictionary* defines *discipline* as "a branch of knowledge or training"; "a particular training routine that develops self-control, learning, or efficiency"; "submission to an authority in order to produce obedience"; "a set of rules for the conduct of a monastic community"; and last, as a "treatment that corrects or punishes." The word is in the same family as *disciple*. Both *discipline* and *disciple* come from the root *discere*, which means "to learn." In the Christian faith, the phrase *spiritual discipline* represents a "practice" of faith that increases one's confidence in and knowledge of God's presence and grace in all of life. Such confidence and knowledge increase hope and the desire to serve God and others.

What does the word *discipline* suggest to you? Look up the the the words *disciple* and *discipline* in a dictionary. What insights do the dictionary definitions offer to your understanding of the words? What connections do you see between *practice* and *discipline*?

Practicing Faith--Responding to God

We don't "save" ourselves by practicing faith. God saves us by grace through faith in the life, ministry, death, and resurrection of

Jesus Christ. Our practice of faith emerges as a grace-filled response to God. God calls for our response because God's desire is that all persons live in the mercy, compassion, justice, peace, and love of God. Paul addressed the tension between what God has done and what we as followers of Jesus do in response to God when he wrote about faith and works represented in the law. His thinking continues to inform what it means to practice our faith as a response to God's grace. Read the following selections of Scripture. Consider what they say to you about what God has done and how God calls you to respond. Write responses to these Scriptures in the space that follows each.

Locate the Nicene Creed, the Apostles' Creed, or another creed in your church's worship resources. Read them. What do they say to you about God? about Jesus? about the Holy Spirit? about how God relates to the world? Write a personal creed. You do not have to show it to anyone unless you want to. Keep your creed handy over the next few weeks of the study. Refer to it in order to see whether you would change it or add anything to it.

"For we hold that a person is justified by faith apart from works prescribed by the law. Or is God the God of Jews only? Is he not the God of Gentiles also? Yes, of Gentiles also, since God is one; and he will justify the circumcised on the ground of faith and the uncircumcised through that same faith. Do we then overthrow the law by this faith? By no means! On the contrary, we uphold the law." (Romans 3:28-31)

"My speech and my proclamation were not with plausible words of wisdom, but with a demonstration of the Spirit and of power, so that your faith might rest not on human wisdom but on the power of God." (1 Corinthians 2:4-5)

"Yet we know that a person is justified not by the works of the law but through faith in Jesus Christ. And we have come to believe in Christ Jesus, so that we might be justified by faith in Christ, and not by doing the works of the law, because no one will be justified by the works of the law." (Galatians 2:16)

"For by grace you have been saved through faith, and this is not your own doing; it is the gift of God—not the result of works, so that no one may boast. For we are what [God] has made us, created in Christ Jesus for good works, which God prepared beforehand to be our way of life." (Ephesians 2:8-10)

Form teams of two or three. Each team choose one of the Scriptures. Discuss what the Scripture says about "practicing" one's faith as a response to God's grace through Jesus Christ. If your group is small, each person can choose a Scripture. Share your insights with the entire group.

"I pray that, according to the riches of his glory, he may grant that you may be strengthened in your inner being with power through his Spirit, and that Christ may dwell in your hearts through faith, as you are being rooted and grounded in love. I pray that you may have the power to comprehend, with all the saints, what is the breadth and length and height and depth, and to know the love of Christ that surpasses knowledge, so that you may be filled with all the fullness of God." (Ephesians 3:16-19)

"The gifts [God] gave were that some would be apostles, some prophets, some evangelists, some pastors and teachers, to equip the saints for the work of ministry, for building up the body of Christ, until all of us come to the unity of the faith and of the

Session 1: What Does Practicing the Faith Mean?

knowledge of the Son of God, to maturity, to the measure of the full stature of Christ. We must no longer be children, tossed to and fro and blown about by every wind of doctrine, by people's trickery, by their craftiness in deceitful scheming. But speaking the truth in love, we must grow up in every way into him who is the head, into Christ, from whom the whole body, joined and knit together by every ligament with which it is equipped, as each part is working properly, promotes the body's growth in building itself up in love." (Ephesians 4:11-16)

Individual and Communal Spiritual Growth

Two of Paul's insights can help our own efforts to "practice" faith. First, Paul recognizes God as the source of our desire to live as Christians. Second, he recognizes that the practices of Christian faith are meant to build the body of Christ. (See Ephesians 4:12.) We practice faith because of God's grace. We practice faith to nurture both our individual spiritual growth and our communal spiritual growth. What we do as Christians affects those around us. God calls individuals and communities of faith into Christian practices.

Looking Ahead

The sessions to come will explore faith practices in several different ways. Sessions 2 through 4 deal with hard questions about life and suffering. Sessions 5 and 6 explore the church, what it is supposed to be and the benefits we can discover as we become a part of the life of a church family. Sessions 7 and 8 explore the meaning and value of experiencing God's presence in the sacraments of Holy Communion and baptism. Sessions 9 through 12 examine ways to get closer to God and several aspects of prayer. Finally, Session 13 looks at Christian commitment. As you engage the topics of the upcoming sessions, you will also gain a deeper sense of the ways practicing the faith can help your faith grow.

Faith Matters for Young Adults: Practicing the Faith

— CLOSING WORSHIP —

Sing again the hymn "Sanctuary," "Cry of My Heart," or another praise chorus or song about wanting to live and worship as a Christian. You can find the songs mentioned above in *The Faith We Sing* (Abingdon Press) or in other books of praise songs and hymns.

Write on your nametag one Christian practice that you want to develop more deeply in your own life. Put your nametag in your billfold or purse so that you can refer to it in the weeks ahead. If you feel moved to do so, talk about this desire with another person in the group or with the entire group.

Pray together the following prayer:
"God of all creation, you have offered life and hope through Jesus Christ. Thank you. Help us to respond to you in ways that will nurture our desire to serve you and one another. We want to practice our faith. Show us how; in Christ we pray. Amen."

Session 2

Is Suffering God's Will?

Pamela Dilmore

FOCUS This session explores God's care and support during times of suffering. It shows how confronting challenging questions about faith can lead to spiritual growth.

– GATHERING –

Greet one another. Sing or read a hymn about assurance in difficult times, such as "There Is a Balm in Gilead," "We'll Understand It Better By and By," or "Precious Lord, Take My Hand."

Find a partner and make a list of challenging questions that you may have as you think about suffering. When you finish, share your questions with the entire group. Make a list of these questions and post the list where all in the group can easily see them. How does the hymn you read or sang respond to the questions raised by suffering?

Pray together the following prayer:
"Good and powerful God, we know that you care for us. We do not know why suffering exists or why good people suffer. Help us to experience growth in our understanding of your love and care for all creation as we explore the hard questions related to suffering; in Christ we pray. Amen."

Engaging the Difficult Questions About Suffering

One faith practice that offers profound opportunities for faith development or Christian spiritual growth is the practice of engaging the difficult questions that emerge from our desire to understand how God relates to human beings and to all creation. One inevitable set of questions for any person who wants to grow in

> **What is your initial response to the questions about God and suffering written in the paragraph and listed during the gathering activity?**

faith emerges from the issues surrounding suffering. Christian tradition teaches us that God is all good and all powerful. God is in control of and cares about all creation. If God is in control of all creation, does that mean God creates and controls suffering? Is suffering God's will? When we experience suffering or see that bad things happen to good people, we may be tempted to ask if God is responsible. What is the role of God in human suffering?

What Is Suffering?

The word *suffer* comes from the Latin *sub*, which means "under," and *ferre*, which means "to bear or to support." *Suffer* has several related meanings:

> **Find a partner. Look at the definitions under "What Is Suffering?" Talk about the ways you understand suffering and the examples you have written. Share the highlights of your conversation with the entire group.**

1. to undergo something unpleasant, such as an injury, grief, loss; to endure, bear, or be afflicted with unpleasantness
2. to undergo an experience or any process or change
3. to allow, permit, or tolerate
4. to bear up under or endure

Write about how you understand suffering in the space below.

List some examples of suffering.

Session 2: Is Suffering God's Will?

Job's Suffering Raises Questions

The Book of Job explores the issue of human suffering. As the book opens, Job, an upright blameless man, enjoys God's blessings in the form of wealth and family harmony. Ha-satan, the accuser in the original Hebrew, is a member of the heavenly council who points out to God that Job has never suffered. The accuser receives permission and power to inflict suffering on Job by killing his children, causing the loss of his material possessions, and afflicting Job with sores all over his body. A blameless man suffers, apparently with God's permission.

The poet struggles with the issue through Job's anger and the attempts of Job's friends to find answers in traditional religious beliefs. The friends believe that wicked people suffer and that righteous people are rewarded. The story raises timeless questions about God's care and human suffering.

Read each of the following Scriptures. Place a mark on the line between "agree" and "disagree" to demonstrate the extent that you agree or disagree with ideas expressed by the various characters.

1. Job 1:21. Job says, "The LORD gave, and the LORD has taken away."
Agree_____Disagree

2. Job 4:7. Eliphaz believes the innocent never perish and the upright are never cut off from God's blessings.
Agree_____Disagree

3 Job. 4:17. Eliphaz doubts that human beings are ever truly innocent or righteous.
Agree_____Disagree

4. Job 8:4. Bildad believes God is punishing Job because Job's children sinned.
Agree_____Disagree

Faith Matters for Young Adults: Practicing the Faith

5. Job 20. Zophar believes God severely punishes the wicked.
Agree_____Disagree

6. Job 33:19. Elihu believes humans are "chastened with pain."
Agree_____Disagree

Job's good friends Eliphaz, Zophar, and Bildad hear of Job's misfortune. They travel from their homes to Job in order to comfort him. At first they sit in the ashes with him in silence for seven days and nights. Finally Job breaks the silence by cursing the day he was born. The friends begin to engage the questions about suffering in their various speeches. Later, another man named Elihu joins the discussion. Look at the following summaries of their points of view:

JOB: My children are dead. My possessions and wealth are gone. My body is covered with sores. I want to die. I maintain my innocence throughout the conversation. I have not sinned.

ELIPHAZ: I am somewhat sympathetic at first. I believe innocent people do not suffer but also wonder who is truly innocent and pure. All people must sin.

BILDAD: God is just. Job's suffering may be caused by his children's sin.

With whom do you identify most? least? Why? Which answer seems most satisfactory? Which one seems least satisfactory? What about each answer makes it acceptable or unacceptable?

ZOPHAR: I am deeply disturbed by Job's anger. I believe God's knowledge is immeasurably greater than human knowledge. God knows every guilt we think we hide. We need to make our hearts right.

ELIHU: I berate Job for what I see as Job's arrogance and pride. I believe firmly that God punishes wickedness.

When Good People Suffer ...

Rodney and Ellie were both musicians who loved bluegrass music. They met at a bluegrass festival, fell in love, got married, and had a little boy named Mike. Both Rodney and Ellie were devout Christians. Even when they were traveling to play at concerts and festivals, they attended church. They loved people and often helped friends and strangers. They were good people who experienced extraordinary suffering.

Ellie was blind. When she was an infant, she had cancer in her eyes. Surgery and radiation treatments saved her life. Friends who knew her were in awe of her ability with any acoustic stringed instrument, especially the hammered dulcimer that Rodney had made for her. They were also amazed at her mothering skills.

Their son Mike was a thriving, happy boy. In a routine check of his eyes, however, doctors found the same kind of lesions in his eyes that had preceded his mother's cancer. The diagnosis came early enough so the lesions were successfully treated with radiation over a period of a year. During that year, Ellie began suffering excruciating sinus headaches. She finally went to see a doctor, who discovered malignant tumors in her sinus cavities. Ellie experienced a great deal of pain and died in a few months.

Rodney was devastated. His parents and his sister gave him emotional support. Friends came to visit often and helped with little Mike's care. Within the next two years, Rodney's sister died of cancer and his mother died from a stroke. Rodney, Rodney's father, and Mike were all that remained of the family.

Consider the following questions. In what ways did Rodney suffer? Ellie? Mike? Rodney's parents? Rodney's sister? What questions do you think Rodney might have asked about his suffering? about Ellie's suffering? about Mike's suffering? How would you explain the cause of their suffering? Do you think their suffering was God's will? Why or why not? What do you think Jesus would have said about their suffering? What do you think Jesus would have done about their suffering? What good, if any, might come from Rodney's suffering? Write your responses in the following space:

Other Biblical Views of Suffering

Ezekiel 18:20-32 places responsibility for suffering squarely on the shoulders of the people of Israel. It draws an analogy to individual responsibility for choices and their consequences. A child shall not suffer for a parent's sin. Nor shall a parent suffer for a child's sin. Everyone's righteousness or wickedness is his or her own. Israel is wrong to say that God is unfair because of the bad things that happen.

Ezekiel stresses Israel's responsibility, calls Israel to get "a new heart and a new spirit," and states that God takes no pleasure in anyone's death (18:31-32). God calls people to turn again to the ways of God. Do not blame God for your suffering. Examine your own spirit and your own heart.

Luke 13:1-5 questions the idea of suffering as punishment and calls all people to turn again to God. Jesus said the Galileans were not worse sinners than his hearers. He used the account of this event to teach that persons are responsible for their actions, that actions have consequences, and that sins can lead to suffering. So people must turn to God.

> Form two teams. Team 1 read Ezekiel 18:20-32 and Team 2 read Luke 13:1-5. What does this Scripture say to you about the role of human beings in suffering? What does this Scripture say to you about the role of God in suffering? What does this Scripture say to you about God's expectations for human beings?

Free Will and Suffering

Human beings were created with free will. We are able to choose what we do. The choices we make have an impact on us and on others. Sometimes our choices, both good and bad choices, cause suffering. Some good choices such as surgery or other medical treatment, depriving a child of something he or she wants, attending a twelve-step program to change some addictive behavior pattern cause suffering. Bad choices such as violent crimes, drunk driving, trespassing, abuse of alcohol and other drugs, sexual promiscuity, inattention to the needs of children or pets, lying, stealing, also cause suffering. Think about the choices you make in daily life and consider the following questions:

Share your definition of *free will* with the entire group. Write a group definition of *free will* using the individual definitions. Discuss connections you see between free will, suffering, and God's care for all creation.

What is human free will?

When does free will cause suffering?

What are some examples of suffering caused by free will?

In what ways can you help those who suffer?

How do you experience or understand God's role as you make choices?

Radical Love

In Matthew 5:43-48 Jesus calls his listeners to a radical, active love. Love our enemies? Pray for those who persecute us? The call to love one's enemies does not mean to love or accept what they do. Loving is different from being a doormat. Allowing others to step on us or abuse us is not love.

Read Matthew 5:43-48. What challenges you about this Scripture? What connections do you see between this Scripture and the reality of human suffering? How does this Scripture offer insight to you about God's role in suffering? about your role? in what way, if any, does it offer hope?

Jesus spoke to a people oppressed by the foreign government of Rome. Jesus' words offer hope to them and to all oppressed people. His teachings offer ways to experience personal power in a powerless situation. One can will good for a human being at the same time one rejects harmful actions that cause suffering. God sends life-giving sunlight and rain on all creation. Human beings within that creation may cause suffering. Their sinfulness does not deny them God's love. Jesus calls human beings to be like God in their capacity to love.

– CLOSING WORSHIP –

Read aloud 1 John 3:1,11. Think about ways you might show love to help people who suffer. Write your ideas below.

Close the session by praying aloud the following prayer or one of your own:
"Caring and loving God, give us faith to believe that in our suffering you suffer with us. Give us courage to reach out to others with love and care in their suffering; in Jesus' name we pray. Amen."

Session 3

Does God Care When I Suffer?

Pamela Dilmore

FOCUS This session will help young adults understand that God does care about persons who suffer and that God's love is constant and universal.

– GATHERING –

Greet one another. Find a partner. Talk about the title of this session, "Does God Care When I Suffer?" How would you answer the question? Share your conversation highlights with the entire group.

Pray together the following prayer:
"God of love, help us as we explore your presence and care for us when we suffer. Guide us as we learn to recognize your presence and care; in Christ we pray. Amen."

God Is With You

Did you ever wonder if God was with you? Did you ever feel the joy of God in the good times and wonder where God was in the bad times? Does God care about you when you suffer?

Plot a lifeline showing the high points and the low points of your life. Illustrate or write a brief sentence telling what each point is on your lifeline.

```
B          T
I          O
R          D
T          A
H          Y
```

What high point stands out in your life? Write more about it.

In what way was God present at that point in your life?

> Form teams of two or three. Discuss your responses to the questions about high points and low points in your life. Take time to pray together if the need arises.

What low point caused you to suffer most in your life? Write more about it.

In what way was God present at that point in your life?

Jesus Cries Out From the Cross

When you are suffering, you might find it difficult to believe that God really cares for you. Did you ever wonder whether you are really important to God? Did you ever ask, "Where are you, God? Why have you abandoned me?" You are in good company. The Gospel of Mark reports that Jesus cried out similar words from the cross (Mark 15:34).

> Read Mark 15:34–37. How do you respond to this story of Jesus' words at the time of his death?

Jesus' words in Mark 15:34 quote the beginning lines of Psalm 22. The psalmist seems to have been suffering from a critical illness and cried out to God for the kind of help given to God's people in the past. Psalm 22 ends with a hymn of praise and a sense of hope in the future. The appeal to both the past and the future offers comfort in the psalmist's present suffering. The psalmist displays a wide range of feeling from despair to hope.

> Read Psalm 22. How does this psalm inform your understanding of Mark 15:34? How does it offer hope?

> Form two teams. Team 1 read Psalm 22 and Team 2 read Psalm 46. Use markers and a long sheet of white paper to create a mural illustrating your psalm.
>
> Discuss: What feelings are communicated in the opening lines of the psalm? Does the psalm look at the past? present? future? What time predominates? What kind of suffering seems to be referred to in the psalm? What feelings are communicated at the end of the psalm? What attitude does the psalm have toward God? In what ways does the psalm express what you have felt about God's presence? In what ways does the psalm challenge you?
>
> After the discussion gather together in the large group. Tell about your mural and how your group answered the questions.

Psalm 46 displays consistent confidence in God, who will be ultimately victorious over the nations. Suffering here takes the form of a battle scene. The psalmist expresses hope in the present tense. God *is* our refuge. God *is* our strength. God *is* our *present* help. God makes wars cease. God breaks bows, shatters spears, and burns shields. This victorious God brings peace and calls the people to "Be still, and know that I am God" (46:10).

Finding God's Care During Suffering

Gladys Dugan: "I know God cares when we suffer. When I lost my son, my question was, 'Where are you, God?' Thirty years ago my son died as the result of an automobile accident. God did not will his death or cause his accident. The accident happened because my son made a bad choice. The weather was bad. He was fifteen years old and talked his friend into letting him drive the car they were in. It was night, and it was raining. The road was slick. This happened before the law required seat belts. If he had had a seat belt on, he might be alive today. He would be forty-five. Anyway, he was going too fast and lost control of the car. It skidded, and he was killed. My husband and I were devastated. We both asked where God was, and we found God in the way people cared. They reached out to us, brought us food, hugged us, cried with us. It was incredible. I don't know what people do who don't have a supportive group of folks around them when bad things happen. I know my years of being in church helped me get through that bad time."

Richard Johnson: "I love basketball, and I really miss it. It's something I did well. I wonder if I will be able to play again. I sometimes ask God why I can't play. My first year of playing in college was great. I was able to start most of the games in the last half of the season. Last summer, I started having severe headaches. I still have them, sometimes for three or four days straight. Doctors found an inoperable tumor in my head. Right now they are treating it with medicine. We are hoping surgery will be possible at some future point. Most of the time I feel OK; but sometimes, well, the pain is bad. God helps us through the bad times. I couldn't endure the pain if God were not with me. My friends are great. The team lets me sit on the bench. I feel grateful for the medical advances, for the doctors and nurses who help me. I thank God for their skill. But I sure do miss playing basketball!"

Tiffany Chun: "I get *so* tired of pinching pennies and clipping coupons. It's really hard to pay bills and put food on the table for my little girl and me. I am a single parent, and my three-year-old daughter and I live in a mobile home that we rent. I'm glad we were able to find something I could afford. Last year, we had to move out of the apartment where we lived because the rent went up. I was scared we might be homeless, and then I found the mobile home. I work the three-to-eleven shift at the hospital, and in the mornings I go to nursing school. I feel really lucky that I can put my little girl in daycare at the hospital while I am at school and at work. It's hard. I'm tired. But things are working.

Session 3: Does God Care When I Suffer?

Doors are opening. We are going to have a better life. When I am with her, I feel God's goodness. I'm lucky to have her and to be able to go to school. When she smiles at me and hugs me, I know God cares for both of us."

Sam Crawford: "Last year, I got beaten up pretty badly by a young man who was robbing my convenience store. I asked myself why did it have to happen to me. I still have to use a cane. I do have a new understanding of what Jesus suffered for me when he was beaten. I feel closer to Jesus now. He was able to forgive those who hurt him so badly. I don't know if I can forgive yet, but God's grace is there for me. I am alive. The young man who beat me is in jail. I want to find some good in this. Maybe God is telling me that my experience might help other victims of crime. I have been thinking about being a volunteer at the victim center. Maybe my experience can help someone else."

> Form four teams. Each team read one of the above stories. Discuss: What kind of suffering is the person in the story experiencing? In what way does this person experience God's care? Tell the entire group about your story and report your responses.

Who Will Separate Us From the Love of Christ?

Romans 8:13-39 is part of Paul's letter to the church at Rome. In it he wrote eloquently about God's love, care, and saving righteousness through Jesus Christ. In Paul's time the Christian life often involved suffering. Paul himself suffered beating, imprisonment, and misunderstanding.

> Read Romans 8:28–39. How might God be working for good in each of the contemporary stories about finding God during suffering? How do these words offer hope for situations of human suffering?

Romans 8 views suffering in light of God's glory (8:18). Paul wrote of the supportive presence of the Spirit who "helps us in our weakness" (8:26). He said, "All things work together for good for those who love God" (8:28). He addressed the difficulty and suffering directly with a question. Paul did not ask, "Does God care when I suffer?" He asked, "Who will separate us from the love of Christ?" (8:35). No suffering of any kind will separate us from God's love.

Paul's insight is astonishing. While most people struggle with whether God cares when we suffer, Paul recognized the reality of suffering and boldly stated that it will not separate us from the love of God in Jesus Christ.

— CLOSING WORSHIP —

Close the session by praying the following prayer or one of your own:
"God of love, we know you truly care. You suffer with us. You love us. You show us ways to get through our suffering. We thank you and praise you. Help us to see, hear, and feel your presence with us in good times and bad times; in the name of the one who suffered for us on the cross and rose again, Jesus the Christ. Amen."

Session 4

What Can I Do to Get Closer to God?

Nancy Regensburger

FOCUS This session will explore Christian spiritual disciplines that will help young adults open themselves to the love and grace of God. They will discover that such practices can lead to growth in love of God, self, and neighbor, both in individuals and in communities of faith.

– GATHERING –

Greet one another. Find a partner. Tell one another about a personal self-discipline. Why do you practice this self-discipline? What, if anything, do you give up as you practice this discipline? What benefits do you gain? Report the highlights of your conversation to the entire group. Make a list of self-disciplines and post it for all to see.

Pray together the following prayer:
"God of love and hope, we know that you care for us. We want to be closer to you even though we know that you are already close to us. Help us and guide us as we explore ways we can open our hearts and minds to your love and grace; in Christ we pray. Amen."

God's Invitation

As Christians, we believe that God accepts and loves each of us and that God invites each of us into a loving relationship. This is indeed a mystery, but we must start here if we are to grow closer to God. John Wesley, the founder of Methodism, taught that God calls us and that we choose to respond in obedience. This summarizes Wesley's understanding of *prevenient grace*. God's grace is reaching out to us, even before we are aware of it. God is never far from each of us. But we must open ourselves to the divine presence.

By what means, then, can we open ourselves to the gift of God's love? The ways by which we may do this are called spiritual disciplines. These are methods of developing our relationship with God in order

> How do you open yourself to the gift of God's love?

that we might respond to God's grace and love. It is important to remember that spiritual disciplines are means only. The end goal of practicing spiritual disciplines is a more loving relationship with self, with others, and especially with God.

Faithful Response to God's Grace

Since we are all unique individuals, we grow spiritually in different ways. Yet Christians over a long period have found some practices to be fundamental and important. Those basic practices are sometimes called the classical disciplines. In the year 1739, eight or ten persons came to John Wesley in London and asked that he spend some time in prayer with them and advise them in spiritual growth. This was the beginning of the United Society, which first gathered in Europe and then in America. The societies were groups who were intentionally seeking the *form* and *power* of godliness, that is how they might be more like God intended them to be as individual Christians and as a community of faith. They united in order to pray together, to receive an encouraging and motivating word from Scripture, and to watch over one another in love, helping one another to live faithfully in response to their salvation. The General Rules of the United Societies required all members to attend upon these ordinances of God:

1. the public worship of God
2. the ministry of the Word, either read or expounded
3. the Supper of the Lord

Session 4: What Can I Do to Get Closer to God?

4. family and private prayer
5. searching the Scriptures
6. fasting or abstinence

Think about each of these. Which ones are most helpful to you? Why? Write about your insights below:

After you have spent time writing about the practices in the list that are most helpful to you, find a partner. Talk together about your written responses. Why do you think the practice of all these ordinances were important for the societies? How do you think it would benefit your faith formation to practice all the ordinances listed?

Pass out Bibles, Bible dictionaries, and concordances. Form six teams. Choose one of the six disciplines to research. Use your own experience, knowledge of Scripture, or any of the resources provided to answer the following questions about each discipline. Prepare a report for the entire group.
1. What does the Bible say about this discipline?
2. How could this discipline be important in developing our relationship with God?
3. What are some specific ways you might practice this discipline?

People Are Different

While the practice of all the six ordinances will help us to grow in faith, it is also true that people worship, read and interpret the Bible, and pray in many ways. People are different. We have preferences. Choosing Christian spiritual disciplines that help us grow closer to God is often an expression of who we are and our unique identities as children of God. We can learn from one another, but each of us has particular gifts and weaknesses, likes and dislikes. God's grace takes a unique shape as it envelops each of us. If praying a particular way helps us grow in love, we should continue to do it. The same is true for worship styles. Some prefer formal worship with written prayers and affirmations, and traditional hymns accompanied by an organ. Others enjoy praise worship with rhythmic music and hand-clapping. These styles of worship as well as other styles are valid. Our call is to worship, and it is certainly a good thing to find a worship style that helps us feel close to God. God calls us to pray, and we can choose from many prayer techniques the ones that best meet our need to feel closer to God.

Because each person's relationship with God is unique, spiritual disciplines should always be freely chosen, never imposed by others. Nor are they something that God requires. Spiritual disciplines are not actions we do to achieve salvation. We do them freely in response to God's love, already freely given. Disciplines never tear us down or become a burden. Rather they help us grow in love of self, others, and God.

Spiritual disciplines bring order to our lives. They can save us from the anxiety and confusion of our disordered desires and our self-centeredness. They provide a sense of stability even when our world seems upside down. And in times when we do not feel close to God, continuing in prayer and other spiritual disciplines keeps us open to a renewal of that relationship.

Spiritual disciplines bring us freedom. They can free us from our attachments to materialism, power, unhealthy relationships, self-ishness, and addictions. In other words, they can free us from sin, which comes between us and God. They can open us to the power of God's redeeming love.

Spiritual Disciplines--Personal and Communal

The practice of Christian spiritual disciplines is both personal and communal. The two aspects cannot be separated. Faith formation and getting closer to God is never simply individualistic. The personal practice of spiritual disciplines leads to growth in the individual's relationship with God and others, thus personal practice is ultimately communal.

Session 4: What Can I Do to Get Closer to God?

IDENTIFYING MY SPIRITUAL DISCIPLINES

List below any activities that you call spiritual discipline. Use enough words to describe each discipline clearly. Be specific. For example, "I pray while I jog three evenings a week."

Fill in the columns after each activity as follows:

In Column A, indicate when the spiritual activity began. (Use C for childhood, T for teen years, R for recently.)

In Column B, estimate how often you now engage in this spiritual discipline.

In Column C, rate from 1 to 5 how important this activity is to you, with 5 being highest in importance.

	A	B	C
ACTIVITY	When begun?	How often?	How important?

Read 1 Corinthians 13. What insights does this Scripture offer to you about the practice of spiritual disciplines?

Growing in Love

We can judge in only one way whether we are growing closer to God. To evaluate our own growth, we ask, Am I becoming more loving? People can have intense religious experiences, speak in tongues, make prophetic statements, and engage in all kind of charity; but if those practices are not done in love, they are all for nothing (1 Corinthians 13).

When a lawyer asked Jesus what the greatest commandment was, he replied, "You shall love the Lord your God with all your heart, and with all your soul, and with all your mind. . . . You shall love your neighbor as yourself" (Matthew 22:34-40). We cannot have one form of love without the other. They are tied together.

> How should we look to Jesus Christ as a source of guidance and for answers in our lives? In what ways does Jesus Christ instruct and advise us with our problems and concerns?

Love of God, of self, and of others follows a circular pattern. As we grow in our awareness of God's acceptance, we value ourselves as individuals loved by God. We also become more involved in loving actions toward others. Love takes form in our lives in compassion, service, stewardship, justice, peace, and so forth. The specific ways in which we live out love in our everyday lives are too many to list. Our love should be evident in the family, in work, in communal activities such as civic and church groups, in political action, in care of the earth, in interpersonal relationships. For example, Christian love may involve wiping a child's messy nose, giving food to a soup kitchen, writing a member of Congress about water pollution or air pollution, or apologizing for hurting another person's feelings.

As we engage in loving actions toward others, we grow closer to God. Jesus said that whenever we feed the hungry, give drink to the thirsty, give a home to strangers, clothe the naked, or visit the sick or those in prison, we do it to him (Matthew 25:42-46). We actually encounter Jesus himself in poor, sick, and oppressed people. Then we have gone full circle, for service has become a means of becoming closer to God.

Spiritual disciplines help us grow closer to God and more accepting of ourselves. They produce loving action in the world. And that love will show itself at every level of our lives—family, work, community, nation, world. In a sense, personal spiritual disciplines are really for the purpose of ministry. If we do not care for our own spiritual selves, we will never do much good for anyone else.

— CLOSING WORSHIP —

Prayerfully consider one *new* spiritual discipline that you would like to try to practice. What is it? How could it help you experience the fact that God is close to you and loves you? How could it benefit those around you?

After a time of silent prayer, close the session with the following prayer:
"Loving God, thank you for offering many ways to grow closer to you. Thank you for the community of faith that teaches us the story of your love and salvation through Jesus Christ. Help us to practice disciplines that will give us a sense of joy, wonder, and commitment as we grow in our love for you and others. Give us the desire to serve you and to serve others in your name; in Christ we pray. Amen."

Session 5

What Is the Church Supposed to Be?

Carol Miller

FOCUS This session explores the nature and purpose of the Christian church and its ministries.

— GATHERING —

Greet one another. As a part of your greeting, tell one another how you define *church*.
Sing or read the hymn "The Church's One Foundation."
Pray together the following prayer:
"God of all people, lead us as we explore what it means to be your people and to be your church; in Christ we pray. Amen."

What Is the Church?

What is the church? A child's hand-game repeats a rhyme that may be familiar to you:

Here is the church.
Here is the steeple.
Open the door.

Here are the people.

What does the word *church* suggest to you? What did you write or draw? Find a partner. Talk together about what you have written or drawn.

We know that church is more than a building. We are getting closer when we think about church as people. Yet, somehow, church is still something more. What is it? For many of us, the word *church* brings to us certain images, ideas, feelings, and memories. Some of these may be positive, and others may be negative. Write or draw in the space below about the images, ideas, feelings, or memories that *church* evokes for you.

What Does the Bible Say?

The Bible has less to say about the religious life of individuals than about the whole people of God as a community. In the Old Testament the people of God are Israel as a nation. Although at times God made covenants with individuals such as Abraham, the content of those covenants meant that God would choose and nurture a *people.* God chose Israel to be God's people, given the task of drawing all nations to God (Isaiah 2:2-3). The New Testament focuses on the Christian community, the church, as the people of God. Beginning as Jesus himself gathered and instructed the disciples, the church was a unity formed by God's Holy Spirit. The church was then commissioned in the world to draw all people to Christ. As the "body of Christ," the church was and continues to be the physical representation of Christ to the world. Individuals matter in the Bible as they are related to the community of faith. Bible study in this session looks at four major biblical images of the church: the people of God, the new creation, the fellowship in faith, and the body of Christ

> Read Isaiah 2:2–4. How does this Scripture about Judah and Jerusalem inform your understanding of church?

The People of God

As God called the nation of Israel to be God's special people of the covenant in the world, so God has called followers of Jesus to be the church. The community of faith exists because God called it into being to fulfill God's purposes. First Peter 2:4-10 speaks of the church in several images, especially "God's own people" (2:9-10). This passage is part of a larger section (1 Peter 1:13–2:10) that urges a Christian community suffering persecution because of their faith in and loyalty to Christ to be holy—pure in their behavior, different from the behavior of other persons. The image of "God's own people" recalls Exodus 19:6 and Hosea 2:23. Romans 9:25-26 also quotes the Hosea passage in talking about how the Gentiles (non-Jews) are God's people in Christ. Write or draw about what the phrase "people of God" suggests to you:

> Read 1 Peter 2:4-10. What does this Scripture say to you about what the church should be or do? In what ways do you see this image present or absent in the church as you know it today?

The New Creation

The image of the church as the new creation helps us think about how God has acted within human history to bring about new possibilities. Faith in Christ makes a real difference in who people become. Two familiar passages that present this image are 2 Corinthians 5:16-21 and Colossians 3:5-11.

Ephesians 2:11-22 develops the theme of how Christ is able to reconcile Jews and Gentiles into "one new humanity" (2:15). A critical issue in the early church was how to receive Gentiles who believed the good news of Jesus Christ. Christianity arose within the Jewish religion. Jews believed that non-Jews were unclean and unholy, unless they converted completely to Judaism. This passage from Ephesians says those old ways of seeing the world with barriers between peoples have been torn down by Christ. Write or draw about what the phrase "the new creation" suggests to you:

> Read Ephesians 2:11-22. What does this Scripture say to you about what the church should be or do? In what ways do you see this image present or absent in the church as you know it today?

The Fellowship in Faith

Various passages throughout the New Testament present glimpses of how Christians are to live together in community as the church. They did not always succeed, but being Christian called for new

> Read Acts 2:41-47. What does this Scripture say to you about what the church should be or do? In what ways do you see this image present or absent in the church as you know it today?

Faith Matters for Young Adults: Practicing the Faith

kinds of behavior and kinship. Acts 2:41-47 presents a picture of the church as the first Christians wanted it to be. Verses 44-45 imply that the early Christians desired a community of shared wealth. Acts 5:1-5 shows how the community put the ideal into practice. Write or draw about what the phrase "fellowship of faith" suggests to you:

The Body of Christ

One of the most powerful images of the church is that of Christ's body on earth. Ephesians 1:15-23 describes the church as "his body, the fullness of" Christ (1:23) and presents a picture of Christ and the church as one person. Christ is the head, and the church is the body. Romans 12:3-8 talks of individuals in the church with different skills as being like the different parts of a human body as they perform different functions. First Corinthians 12:4-26 offers a longer discussion of the same theme. Write or draw about what the phrase "the body of Christ" suggests to you:

Read Romans 12:3-8. What does this Scripture say to you about what the church should be or do? In what ways do you see this image present or absent in the church as you know it today?

An Imperfect Church in an Imperfect World

Because the church consists of fallible human beings, it is by no means perfect. Yet, much would be missing from our world without the church. Formed by the Holy Spirit, the church has power.

God created the church to be God's servant community in the world, drawing all people to God. Since God gives the church, the church continues to grow and to work on its human imperfections until it becomes what God calls it to be.

What should the church do and be? If we look at the church using the biblical image of the body of Christ and asking some questions, Jesus can inform what we think the church should do and be. Read the following questions and list specific places, activities, or people as answers:

Form teams of two or three. Invite each team to design a poster for your local church (or the entire Christian church) that depicts the church's strengths in a way that would encourage people to join. Hang the posters on the meeting room walls. Ask someone in each team to tell the entire group about the poster. Make a list of the things you believe the church does right. What does the church offer that nothing else offers? What would be missing from the world if the church did not exist? What difference can these lists make in our understanding of the church?

1. If Jesus were physically present today, where would he be found?

2. If Jesus were physically present today, what would he be doing?

3. If Jesus were physically present today, with whom would he associate?

A Community of Faith? Why Not Go It Alone?

"Why should I go to church? I experience God in nature. When I see a sunset or a mountain or the sea, I experience God's presence. I can worship God alone. I don't need a church." Certainly, these words point to the reality of God through Christ in all creation. God is much more than either church or the created world. But church is about community. Below is a specific list pointing to the value of church as God intended it to be. Read each item on the list and the Scripture that follows it. Write about any insights you gain from your reading. Share your ideas with the entire group.

Witness. The church is to be a stage or a showcase that allows the world to see what it means for God to be with God's people (John 13:35).

Support. The Christian faith lives in a hostile environment. We need one another for support and should encourage one another in our Christian life (Galatians 6:2).

What characteristics of the church make you want to be a part of it? What characteristics might keep you away? What does the church do that individuals could not do alone?

Instruction. We need the church to instruct us. We need to be able to discuss and evaluate our faith with other Christians (1 Thessalonians 5:12-13).

Fellowship. When we all share the same love and have the same center for our lives, we want to be with one another. We understand one another as no one else does (1 Corinthians 1:2).

Worship. We need corporate worship in which we confess together, affirm our common faith, pray for one another, commune with God as a fellowship, hear the gospel, receive the sacraments, and form a witness that points to God (1 Corinthians 14:26).

Service. We can accomplish together, as a congregation and as a denomination, tasks we could never do alone (mission projects, building hospitals and shelters, and so forth (Acts 2:44).

We Are All One in Christ

The hymn "In Christ There Is No East or West" reminds us that all Christians everywhere are bound together in "one great fellowship of love." Perhaps this image comes closest to expressing what the church is supposed to be as the people of God, as the new creation, as the fellowship of faith, and ultimately, as the body of Christ. Each of us as an individual Christian has the opportunity to participate in making the vision in the song a reality.

— CLOSING WORSHIP —

Sing the hymn "In Christ There Is No East or West." Close the session with the following prayer:
"Loving God, bind us together in your infinite love. Help us to be your people, your church, so that all can know you. Help us to serve you and others; in Christ we pray. Amen."

Session 6

Why Should I Go to Church?

Carol Miller

FOCUS This session will help persons consider and respond to opportunities for worship, service, and faith development within a church family.

– GATHERING —

Greet one another. Find a partner and tell one another how you would answer the question, "Why Should I Go to Church?" Make a list of responses for the group to see.

Pray together the following prayer:
"God, in the power of your Spirit, you bring us together through Jesus Christ. Help us as we explore what it can mean in our lives to participate in the life of a church family; in Christ we pray. Amen."

We Are the Church

Why should I go to church? Perhaps you have asked the question. Can't we worship outside the church? Yes, but ... the church is the community of faith brought together as followers of Jesus Christ and empowered by the Holy Spirit to grow and to help others grow in love of God and neighbor. Actually in one sense, as Christians, we do not "go to" church; we *are* the church. We gather together to worship God and to serve God.

Many persons on the fringes of the church, and even some who are closely connected to the church, hold an idea of the church as a spiritual grocery store. The church exists "out there," independently of them. Unless they have some need the

How do you define the *church*?

church might fill, they ignore the church. When some need arises, then they can choose to go to church. We, and our need, can never be the focal point of the church. God, revealed in Jesus Christ, is the focal point. By putting God's will first as we live as part of the church, we find our needs are met as well (Matthew 6:33). The church is composed of servants. We might compare the church to a family. Or we might think of it as a cohesive work setting where all the workers feel a sense of ownership and pride in what they accomplish together. Yet, the church is more than a family and more than a cohesive work setting. The church is, according to Paul, the body of Christ (1 Corinthians 12:27).

What Do I Have to Give to the Church?

First Corinthians 12:1-31. The New Testament uses the metaphor of the church as the body of Christ in several places. It is most completely developed by Paul in 1 Corinthians 12:1-31. A similar but briefer passage is Romans 12:3-16.

What kinds of gifts are mentioned in 1 Corinthians 12:27-28 and Romans 12: 4-8? How are these gifts expressed in your own congregation? Write your name on an index card. All group members place the cards in a basket. Choose a card with someone else's name on it. Write on that card one gift helpful to the church they think that group member has. Give it to the person whose name is on the card. Discuss your response to the gift that is written on your card.

As a body, the Christian community should function as a whole. Its parts should work together. Each member of the Christian community should recognize, honor, and work with every other member. Persons arrive within the church because God has called them. Just as God has arranged the human body in such a way that each part has a function, so the individual members of the church have a function.

Paul considers qualities such as generosity, kindness, and an encouraging spirit as gifts given by the Holy Spirit for the sake of building up the church. The congregation needs to understand that all people have gifts to offer, not just those persons blessed with special skills. Not all gifts are skills that require formal training. Listening, compassion, generosity, and the ability to work hard are as valuable as any of the other gifts listed.

Read the following Scriptures. In the space provided, write or draw about how the Scripture informs your understanding of what you might offer to the church. What are your gifts?

1 Corinthians 12:27-28

Romans 12:4-8.

Finding Your Niche

The key to experiencing Christian community in a local congregation often lies in finding a niche, a place where you can be known and get to know others while you are offering your gifts and your work to God. Where might that niche be for you in your present congregation? Write your reflections in the space below.

What do you do if no group exists that will offer you the opportunity you need for Christian fellowship and service? Perhaps you can help to create a new niche, for others as well as for your-selves. If you feel a lack, others probably feel the same way. What could you do to start a group that will help you serve Jesus Christ in and through this congregation? Write your reflections in the space below.

"A Want Ad"

If we could secure good members by putting an advertisement in a newspaper, how would we advertise? Use the guide below to write an ad:

Wanted:

Qualifications:

Must be willing to:

Experience needed:

Salary:

Chance for advancement:

"Perks":

Need not apply if:

After you have written your want ad, create a consensus ad for the entire group by recording responses on a large sheet of paper. When the group advertisement is complete, discuss these questions: How would this ad work if placed in the newspaper? What qualifications does a church member need to have? Would you feel qualified to apply? Why or why not? How do you think God would write the ad?

Fortunately, we come to the body of Christ because of God's grace rather than because of our personal qualifications! God loves us. God offers *all* people salvation, love, and hope. When we go to church and participate in its ministries, we participate in God's ongoing work through Jesus Christ. We do so out of

Session 6: Why Should I Go to Church?

gratitude for what God has already done and continues to do through Christ.

What Does the Church Have to Give to You?

Churches are not perfect, however, churches are empowered by the Spirit to form people into the image of God in Jesus Christ and to offer the good news of salvation, renewal, love, mercy, and hope through Jesus Christ. In Paul's letters to the churches in Philippi and Ephesus, we catch a glimpse of what the church can give.

The Mind of Christ

Philippians 2:1-11. The Philippian church was a congregation that existed in a challenging time. Paul wrote to them from prison. Acts 16 says that Paul and Silas were jailed in Philippi. Probably the Christian community at Philippi continued to suffer persecution. In Philippians 2 Paul warned the Philippian Christians against forces inside the church that could threaten the community of faith. Paul warned against thinking too highly of oneself and one's gifts. He points to the self-emptying love of Christ as the example for the behavior of believers (2:5-8). To encourage the Philippians toward a more humble attitude, Paul reminded them of this early Christian hymn that extolled Christ Jesus' humility.

Read Philippians 2:1-11. In the space below, write or draw about any insights the Scripture offers about what the church can offer.

Unity in Christ

Ephesians 2:11-22: The Letter to the Ephesians addresses new Christians who had been pagans. They had been "far off" from

God (2:13); they did not know the one true God. Now, in Christ, they do know God, and so they have been "brought near" (2:13).

Christians, both former pagans and Jewish Christians, find reconciliation with God and with one another by their union with Christ.

The writer of Ephesians said that whether new Christians were Jews or pagans, they are all one in Christ now. Race, nation, and background mean nothing. All the things that divide people are destroyed by their unity in Christ. This is an important message for today's church.

> Form teams of two or three. Read aloud Philippians 2:1-11 and Ephesians 2:11-22. Discuss what you wrote or drew in response to these Scriptures. What makes the church different from other worthy organizations?

Read Ephesians 2:11-22. In the space below, write or draw about any insights the Scripture offers about what the church can offer.

The Church's One Foundation

A hymn familiar to many who worship and participate in the ministries of a church is "The Church's One Foundation." It tells about Jesus Christ as the foundation and about those who follow Christ as a new creation, in union with God through Christ. Locate other songs about the church in a hymnbook. Some suggestions are

"O Church of God, United"
"Blest Be the Tie That Binds"
"We Are the Church"
"Help Us Accept Each Other"
"O Zion, Haste"
"God of Grace and God of Glory"

"Lord, Whose Love Through Humble Service"
"Lord, You Give the Great Commission"
"The Church of Christ, in Every Age"
"When the Church of Jesus"

What does the hymn say about the purpose of the church? In what ways, if any, does the hymn speak about how church members should care for the world or for one another? What is the main message about the church in this hymn? Write about or draw your responses below:

A Covenant

You have gifts to offer to the church; and the church has something to offer to you. Based upon what you have explored so far, what do you think should go in a covenant—a mutual agreement—between a church and its members? Respond to the following questions:

What should a member of the church be willing to promise?

Record responses to the covenant questions on a chalkboard or a large sheet of paper. Do you think your group's version of the covenant would work within your congregation? Why or why not?

What should the Christian church promise to the member?

What should members expect from their local congregations?

Such a covenant makes most sense when we remember what Paul said about our identities as Christians. As the church we "are the body of Christ and individually members of it." Claiming this reality gives a renewed perspective on what it means to "go" to church. The more we "go" to church, the more likely we are to recognize that we "are" the church.

— CLOSING WORSHIP —

Sing or read aloud the hymn "Blest Be the Tie That Binds." What do the words to this hymn say to you about reasons for going to church? What insights have you gained from this session about what church is or what church can be? How do you think you can become more involved in the ministry of Christ through the church?

Pray silently about your commitment to church. Close the session by praying the Lord's Prayer.

Session 7

What Does Baptism Mean?

Pamela Dilmore

FOCUS This session will explore God's gift of baptism and what it tells us about God, the church, and the Christian life.

– GATHERING –

Ahead of time prepare a worship center. Put a candle in a candleholder and matches in the worship center. Put some clear glass stones or pebbles into a glass bowl. Enough stones should be available for all in the group to have one. Place a pitcher of water near the glass bowl. You will use the bowl of pebbles and the pitcher of water in the closing worship.

Greet one another. Sing or read the words to a baptismal hymn such as "We Know That Christ Is Raised," "This Is the Spirit's Entry Now," or "Come, Let Us Use the Grace Divine." Find a partner. Discuss what the hymn says to you about the meaning of baptism.

Tell one another about your baptism if you have been baptized or about your understanding of baptism if you have not been baptized.

Pray together the following prayer:
"God of hope and new life, be with us as we explore the meaning of baptism. Help us to hear again the message of hope it proclaims; in Christ we pray. Amen."

Initiation Into God's Family in Christ

Since the Pentecost experience in Acts 2, baptism has been practiced by Christians as a ritual of entry into the church (Acts 2:37-42). In Matthew 28:18-20, Jesus tells his followers to "make disciples of all nations, baptizing them in the name of the Father and of the Son and of the Holy Spirit, and teaching them to obey everything that I have commanded you." Through baptism, disciples enter Christ's family and choose to learn and act according to Christ's teaching and example. In so doing, believers participate in personal faith development and the faith development of all others in the family.

> Read Acts 2:37-42. What does this Scripture say to you about baptism? about repentance? about the gifts of forgiveness and the power of the Holy Spirit? about life as a Christian?

Jesus' Baptism and God's Kingdom

Our Christian tradition of baptism as a sign of our initiation into the family of God in Christ is deeply rooted in ancient Jewish traditions. Cleansing or washing with water was an important purity ritual before entering the Temple. Proselytes, those who chose to become Jews, were often baptized. Both purity and welcome into God's family are recognized and celebrated in Christian baptism. We recognize what God has done to save us in Christ and that we are God's children welcomed into and nurtured by the family of Christ.

> Read the accounts of Jesus' baptism in Mark 1:9-11; Matthew 3:13-17; Luke3:21-22; and John 1:29-24. What do these Scriptures say to you about God's work through Jesus? about Jesus' understanding of his mission? What connections do you make between Jesus' baptism and baptism in the church as we practice it today?

Baptism also signifies our recognition of God's kingdom. John the Baptizer called for the people to repent and be baptized in anticipation of God's coming kingdom. When Jesus submitted to baptism by John, it was an occasion that revealed him as God's Son rather than Jesus' personal need to repent and to be forgiven. Jesus' baptism as recorded in Mark 1:9-11, Matthew 3:13-17, and Luke 3:21-22 as well as in John 1:29-34 presents him as the Anointed One, the Son of God, who would establish the Kingdom. Mark, Matthew, and Luke include a quotation drawn from Psalm 2:7 and Isaiah 42:1. In Mark and Luke the quotation is "You are my Son, the Beloved; with you I am well pleased" (Mark 1:11; Luke 3:22). The dove mentioned in all four Gospels is also a key image in the renewed creation after the flood in the story of Noah (Genesis 8:8-12). Thus Jesus is "baptized" into his mission to inaugurate God's kingdom as the Anointed One, the Messiah.

God's Gift and Our Response

The ritual of baptism can be viewed as a mini-gospel in and of itself because it represents God's gifts of life, salvation, forgiveness, hope, and power through Jesus Christ. In addition it provides the occasion for our response to God's gift. God's love, care, and power intertwined with human response through the family of Christ. Baptism is a beginning of the Christian life in the community of faith.

> How do you understand God's grace? How do you think God's influence can find expression in our daily lives?

The practice of baptism is God's gift. Lawrence Hull Stookey in *Baptism: Christ's Act in the Church* affirms that words and actions of the ritual tell the story of God's grace given through creation, covenant, Christ, church, and the coming Kingdom. In the New Testament, the word that is translated "grace" suggests "gift," "joy," "favor," "benefit," and the influence of God on the human heart, an influence that finds expression in our daily lives.

Baptism is also our response to God's grace, but it is never an individualistic ritual. Through participation in baptism, we, as the church and as individual Christians, recognize that through Jesus Christ we belong to the family of God. We understand and celebrate that we are a part of a community of faith that nurtures us and contributes to our growth in faith. Baptism is intimately related to the community of faith throughout time, the community that came before us, that nurtured us, and that will continue after us.

Baptism gives the community of faith an opportunity to offer praise and thanksgiving for

How do you see the role of the church in the lives of baptized Christians? What role has the church played in your faith journey? If you have not been involved in the life of a church family, what role might it play? What role has it played in the life of someone you know?

what God has done and what God will continue to do through Christ. It also gives the opportunity for the church to recognize and reclaim its commitment to nurture the faith development of the person being baptized. If we were baptized as infants, we recognize that God's grace precedes us and flows through the community of faith to us. If we made our own profession of faith at our baptism, we recognized, accepted, and responded to God's active grace in our lives and in the community of faith.

When we are baptized or when we remember and celebrate our baptism, we accept and claim the gospel story and the invitation to new life. We repent or turn again to God who forgives us and makes us new people in Christ. We die to the old life and rise again to new life in Jesus Christ. Washed clean, raised with Christ, and incorporated into the family of God through Christ, we claim the hope of God's kingdom both in our midst and in the future. Through baptism we celebrate that God's grace precedes us, enfolds us, offers hope for the future, and invites our response of gratitude. We affirm the commitment to love and serve God and others through Christ. Think about the phrase *new life*. In the following space, write or sketch about what *new life* suggests to you.

Water and Words

Baptism is a ritual that involves both words and water. In most rituals, the words talk about our initiation into the family of God, God's salvation, and new birth through water and the Spirit. They ask about our willingness to renounce evil, to repent, and to accept God's freedom and power to resist all forms of evil, injustice, and oppression. They give the opportunity to express trust in Jesus Christ as Savior. They invite sponsors and parents to commit to the nurture of the candidate through teaching and example and to encourage them in their faith development. The church is invited to reaffirm its faith in Christ. A prayer recalls images in both the Old and New Testaments that point to God's saving grace in the Creation, in the covenant with Noah, in the birth and baptism of Jesus, and in the power and presence of the Holy Spirit.

At this point, the person is baptized with water in one of three ways: immersion, pouring, or sprinkling. Those around the baptized person—pastor, sponsors, and family members—lay their hands on the candidate and invoke God's Holy Spirit to empower the person to become a faithful disciple of Jesus Christ. The community of faith welcomes the newest member of Christ's family.

> Locate the ritual for baptism in the worship resources of your church. Read the ritual. What does it say about God? about Jesus Christ? about the person who is being baptized? about the community of faith?

Water is basic to life. Without water there would be no life as we know it. Water has the power to cleanse, to nurture life, and to destroy. In the space below make a list of the characteristics of water.

The use of water in baptism generates meaningful symbolism from the various characteristics of water and underscores the words that refer to the biblical accounts of the Creation, the Flood, and the birth and baptism of Jesus. God's spirit moves over the waters at Creation (Genesis 1:1-2). The destructive flood waters in the story of Noah cleanse the earth, and God establishes a renewed creation and a covenant with Noah (Genesis 5–9). Jesus is revealed as the Son of God when John baptizes him (Mark 1:4-11; Matthew 3:1-17; Luke 3:1-22). Other biblical references using water echo in the symbol. In the story of the Exodus, God's people are delivered from the Egyptians as God parts the waters of the sea (Exodus 14:1-29). God commands Moses to strike a rock in order to provide water for the people who are complaining of thirst (Exodus 17:1-6). God's power through Jesus is clear when Jesus calms the seas (Matthew 8:24-27) and walks on the water (Matthew 14:22-33). In John's Gospel, Jesus has conversation with a Samaritan woman and during their conversation refers to himself as "living water" (John 4:5-15). In all these biblical stories, and in others as well, water is a deeply meaningful image associated with God's creating, saving, cleansing, and regenerating power.

> What connections do you make with these various images of water, the power and activity of God, and baptism?

Read each of the following Scriptures. In the space provided, write about the water in the Scripture. What quality or characteristic of water informs this Scripture? What does the water suggest about God's power?

Genesis 1:1-10

Genesis 7:1-10

Genesis 9:1-17

Exodus 14:1-29

Exodus 17:1-6

Matthew 8:24-27

Matthew 14:22-33

John 4:5-15

Life in the Family of Christ

In this session we have explored God's gift of baptism as a ritual of initiation into the family of Christ, and we have discovered that baptism celebrates much more. Baptism signifies what God has done and continues to do for us through Jesus Christ, our response to God's gift and to God's word of hope in Jesus Christ, and what God continues to do as we look forward to the full expression of God's kingdom now and in our future. To be baptized is to claim our identities as children of God, beloved of God and called of God, through Christ, to grow in love and service toward God and neighbor.

— CLOSING WORSHIP —

Gather at the worship center. Light the candle. Spend a moment of silent prayer offering thanks to God for the gift of baptism and all that it means. During the silent prayer, someone pour the water slowly over the pebbles in the glass bowl. Listen prayerfully to the sound of the water as it is poured. After all the water has been poured over the pebbles, take your own pebble from the water. When everyone has taken a pebble, pray together the Lord's Prayer. Keep your pebble with you as a reminder of your identity as a child of God in the family of Christ.

Session 8

What Does Holy Communion Mean?

Pamela Dilmore

FOCUS This session will help young adults explore the Christian service of the Lord's Supper, its scriptural backgrounds, and what it can mean to faith development.

- GATHERING

Greet one another. Sing the hymn "Let Us Break Bread Together." Find a partner. Locate another hymn in your church hymnal about Holy Communion, Eucharist, or the Lord's Supper. Talk about what the text of the hymn says about the meaning of the ritual. Share the highlights of your conversation with the entire group.

Pray together the following prayer:
"Lord of life, salvation, and hope, enrich our understanding as we explore Holy Communion. Help us sense your presence and experience renewed meaning through this study; in Christ we pray. Amen."

Sacraments

Holy Communion, also called the Eucharist and the Lord's Supper, is one of the two sacraments recognized by Protestant Christians. The other is baptism. Traditionally, the church has understood a sacrament to be a ritual or a practice that provides a participant a special opportunity to experience God's grace. St. Augustine described a sacrament as a "visible form of an invisible grace." The word originally referred to creeds, the Lord's Prayer, and other practices. The Eastern Church and the Roman Catholic Church recognize seven sacraments today: baptism, confirmation, the Eucharist, penance, extreme unction, orders, and matrimony. Protestants recognize baptism and Holy Communion as sacraments because the Gospels report that these were instituted by Jesus.

Names for Holy Communion

Most Christians use one of three different names for the sacrament of Holy Communion, and each of the names says something meaningful about the ritual.

(1) Holy Communion—The words *Holy Communion* bring to mind and heart the sense of unity in Christ. Its focus is on the communal nature of the service and of the church, which is all one in Christ. Through participation in the sacrament, we discover unity with God and with one another in Christ.

(2) Eucharist—The word *Eucharist* is a transliteration of the Greek word for "thanksgiving." At the heart of this word is the root word *charis*, which carries several meanings. Some of the meanings are "gift," "grace," "joy," "pleasure," and "thanks." It reminds the participant that the service of the Eucharist is a time to offer

> Which of the ways of referring to the service of Holy Communion is most familiar to you? Which one has the most meaning for you? Why?

thanks to God, and it recalls that Jesus gave thanks at the institution of the meal.

(3) Lord's Supper—This designation for the holy meal comes from Paul's reference to the meal in 1 Corinthians 11:20. It helps us place the meal in the context of table fellowship that was such a vital part of Jesus' ministry. It also suggests the last meal Jesus shared with the disciples before his death and the hope of the messianic banquet in God's kingdom.

In Roman Catholic tradition, Holy Communion is one part of the Mass. The word *mass* comes from the Latin word meaning "to send." Roman Catholic Christians use this word to refer to their liturgy, which is made up of two main parts: the Liturgy of the Word (including readings from both the Old and New Testaments, the homily, and the creed) and the Liturgy of the Eucharist (including the great eucharistic prayer and consecration, the prayer that Christ taught—the Lord's Prayer, and Holy Communion).

"This Is My Body"

The Institution of the meal that came to be known as Holy Communion, the Eucharist, and the Lord's Supper can be found in four Scriptures. The Gospels of Matthew, Mark, and Luke talk about the last supper with Jesus and the disciples as being a Passover meal. (Matthew 26:26-28; Mark 14:22-24; and Luke 22: 17-20). In Jewish tradition, the Passover meal recalls God's deliverance of the enslaved people in the Exodus. Thus God's saving power permeated the atmosphere of meaning that surrounded Jesus and the disciples in these three Gospels. In his letter to the church at Corinth, Paul addressed abuses at the Lord's Supper by reminding them of Jesus' words (1 Corinthians 11:23-25).

In each of these Gospels and in Paul's letter, the bread and wine are associated with the body and blood of Jesus. They point to the sacrificial death of Jesus. They also point to the hope beyond death because they mention Jesus' presence after his death. In Matthew Jesus says he will drink new wine with the disciples in his Father's kingdom. In Mark's version, they will drink new wine in the kingdom of God. Luke says that Jesus will not drink until the kingdom of God comes. Paul reminds the church at Corinth in 1 Corinthians 11:26 that drinking the cup proclaims Jesus' death "until he comes."

Read each of the following Scriptures. What key ideas are present? How are they the same? How are they different? Write about your insights in the space provided.

1 Corinthians 11:23-25

Matthew 26:26-28

Mark 14:22-24

Luke 22:17-20

Celebration by the Early Christian Community

Acts 2:41-46 offers an idyllic glimpse of the communal practices of the early church. These Scriptures speak of breaking bread, prayers, and a joyous sense of gratitude. "They devoted themselves to the apostles' teaching and fellowship, to the breaking of bread and the prayers," and "day by day, as they spent much time together in the temple, they broke bread at home and ate their food with glad and generous hearts, praising God and having the goodwill of all the people" (2:42, 46-47a). Acts 20:7 shows that breaking bread was a regular practice. "On the first day of the week, when we met to break bread, Paul was holding a discussion with them" (20:7a). Read Acts 2:41-46 and 20:7a and make notes in the space pro-

> How do the scenes of life among the early believers in Acts 2:41-46 and 20:7 compare to the communal life of your local church? to the rite of Holy Communion?

vided about any insights they offer to you about Holy Communion and the worship life of the community.

Acts 2:41-46

Acts 20:7a

Bread and Wine--Body and Blood

The substances consumed during the ritual of Holy Communion are bread and either grape juice or wine. In the Gospels of Mark, Matthew, and Luke the bread represents the body of Jesus and the grape juice (fruit of the vine) or wine represents the blood of Jesus. Many Christians serve grape juice rather than wine in order to avoid the issues related to the use or abuse of alcohol.

Read John 6:25-58. What does this Scripture say to you about God? about Jesus? about the followers of Jesus? about the practice of Holy Communion in the early church and in your local church? What, if anything, challenges you about the Scripture? Why?

What do you think Jesus is trying to communicate in this conversation with the disciples?

John 6:25-58 shows the importance of bread in the memory of the people. After feeding the five thousand, Jesus conversed with the disciples. He told them, "Do not work for the food that perishes, but for the food that endures for eternal life, which the Son of Man will give you. For it is on him that God the Father has set his seal" (6:27). The disciples asked for a sign to help them believe. They told Jesus, "Our ancestors ate the manna in the wilderness; as it is written, 'He gave them bread from heaven to eat' " (6:31). Jesus connected with this memory by pointing to God. "Very truly, I tell you, it was not Moses who gave you the bread from heaven, but it is my Father who gives you the true bread from heaven. For the bread of God is that which comes down from heaven and gives life to the world" (6:32-33). He went one step further to identify God's work through him. "I am the bread of life. Whoever comes to me will never be hungry, and whoever believes in me will never be thirsty" (6:35). God's work through Jesus thus connected with key memories of the people and with the life-giving, nourishing qualities of bread. John's Gospel, which probably reflects the practice of the early church, mentions the gift of eternal life that comes through eating the flesh and drinking the blood of the Son of Man. (See 6:53-58.) A key idea here for Christians is that to participate in Holy Communion is to share divine life in relationship with God and with other people.

The Great Thanksgiving

Gratitude to God is a key part of the ritual of Holy Communion in Christian tradition. As we saw earlier, another name for Holy Communion is *Eucharist*, which actually means "thanksgiving." Most Christians will hear a prayer offered over the bread and cup, which contains a "remembering" of God's redemptive activity in Jesus Christ, the story of Jesus' institution of the meal during the Last Supper, and a request for the Holy Spirit to be present. Look at the worship resources for Holy Communion in your church. How are these three parts included? How do they connect with thanksgiving? Write about or draw images that reflect any insights you gain.

Hope in the Risen Christ

Participation in Holy Communion, Eucharist, or the Lord's Supper provides opportunities to experience and to reflect upon hope for the future through the resurrected Christ. In the Resurrection appearance in Luke 24:30-43, the disciples recognized the risen

Read Luke 24:13–35. How does this Scripture offer hope? What connections do you see to the experience of Holy Communion?

Christ during table fellowship. "When he was at the table with them, he took bread, blessed and broke it, and gave it to them. Then their eyes were opened, and they recognized him" (24:30-31). They commented to one another about how their hearts burned as Christ opened the Scriptures on the road to Emmaus, and they told others "how he had been made known to them in the breaking of the bread" (24:32, 35).

A Story of God's Love

Holy Communion is so much more than a memory of Jesus' sacrificial death. It certainly recalls what Jesus gave to us through his death, but it is also a story of how God's love and work continue through Jesus Christ. It points to and calls us to participate in the life and hope of God today and in our future.

— CLOSING WORSHIP —

Plan to attend a worship service in your church that offers Holy Communion. Offer a prayer of gratitude to God for Holy Communion and what it can mean in a person's life and faith development.

Session 9

What Should I Do With What I Have?

Carol Miller

FOCUS This session will help young adults to examine what Christian faith teaches about values and attitudes related to money and possessions.

— GATHERING —

Sing the hymn "Seek Ye First." Find a partner and discuss how this hymn informs attitudes or values toward money and the accumulation of possessions.

Pray together the following prayer:
"God of all creation, we thank you for what we have. Teach us your priorities as we explore what we can do with our money and our possessions; in Christ we pray. Amen."

What Possessions Mean

Anyone who works full-time in this society has money and possessions. The question of whether a Christian should have money and possessions is not valid unless some alternative, such as a communal style of living, could provide for one's needs. Jesus and his disciples had money (Judas served as treasurer, John 12:4-6). The important questions for Christians in the United States today are what to do with what we have and what attitudes we should have toward money and possessions.

Money and other possessions can fill many roles in a person's life. Often those roles are inappropriate for Christians. Sometimes people feel that money and possessions provide security, giving a feeling of self-worth, or allow them to feel superior. When possessions fill such roles in a person's life, they take on exaggerated importance. They easily become gods in the sense that they are so important to life that one cannot let go of them. But for Christians, a better role for money and possessions is to use them as tools to accomplish God's goals and to sustain God's servants.

Find a partner and compare your rankings of the meaning of possessions. What did you add to the list? What else do you think needs to be on the list? Why?

With the exception of those possessions that are needed to sustain life, what do you think possessions mean to most people? Rank the following reasons people value possessions in order of importance to you. Add any other reasons you think should be included with these.

__ social equality
__ value as a person
__ feeling of belonging
__ feeling of being loved
__ feeling of security
__ social superiority
__ sign of power
__ sign that we are due respect

This session does not argue whether having things is right or wrong. Instead, it focuses on money and possessions from a Christian point of view. Christians in our society usually have some money and possessions. The question for Christians is how to handle and control what we have.

As you become more particularly aware of your own attitudes about money and possessions, you may feel somewhat defensive. If you are struggling between the claims of society and the claims of Christ, be honest about that struggle with the others in your group. You will probably discover that others have similar struggles.

Manna From Heaven

In Exodus 16:13-24, the Hebrews, whom God had rescued from Egyptian slavery, had been wandering in the desert. They had grumbled and complained ever since God delivered them from Pharaoh. They did not feel safe trusting in God. They only felt safe when they gathered enough "things" around them to make them feel secure about the future.

> Read Exodus 16:13-24. What does this Scripture say to you about accumulation and hoarding? What does it say to you about trusting God's provision?

This Scripture describes their complaint because they did not see where they would get food in the desert. When God provided manna for them to eat, they tried to hoard it. They did not want to trust God day by day. If God allowed them to stockpile the food, they would transfer their trust and worship from the God who really was saving them to the stockpile of food, which could not save them. God caused the surplus food to rot so the people would learn to trust only God. This story has a direct connection to our desire to accumulate things and then to treat them as objects of ultimate trust, as gods.

Do Not Worry

In Luke 12:22-34, Jesus made a similar point to the one demonstrated in the story in Exodus of God's provision of manna from heaven. He seemed to make a case against attending to the daily provisions of life. On closer reading, however, we can see that Jesus was saying something much more profound about human anxiety, having what we need, and God's care and provision. Read Luke 12:22-34. Write your responses to the following questions:

What challenges you about this teaching of Jesus?

What does Jesus seem to be saying about having what we need?

What is he saying about God?

A Rich Young Man and a Tax Collector

In Matthew 19:16-24 the rich young man needed to sell all his possessions because, as Jesus saw the situation, the man's money and possessions had become his god. The young man showed this to be true when he chose to keep all his possessions rather than become a follower of Jesus. He asked for the secret of eternal life. But having been given it, he rejected it in favor of his wealth.

Read Matthew 19:16-24 and Luke 19:1-10. How are the rich man and Zacchaeus the same? How are they different Which man do you admire most? least? why? What do these Scriptures say to you about the values that surround money?

In Luke 19:1-10, Zacchaeus, a hated tax collector who had increased his wealth at the expense of his own people, promised to give away half of all he owned and make reparations from part of the rest of his wealth. Jesus said nothing about Zacchaeus giving up all of his possessions, as he said to the rich young man. Zacchaeus apparently gave up worshiping wealth.

Supporting Self and Helping Others

Ephesians 4:28 gives the two legitimate uses of money for the Christian: to support oneself and to help others, especially the poor. Proverbs 30:7-9 gives a rationale for keeping money in balance in this life. Persons should have an honorable way of caring for themselves and their families without having so much that they feel independent of God. When possessions pile up, persons too easily let them become objects of trust.

Luke 12:13-21, the parable of the rich fool, illustrates well what misusing wealth means. This person literally piled up possessions and put his trust in them, saying, "Relax, eat, drink, be merry" (12:19). He failed to look for God's will. In fact, he could not think of anything else to do with his goods except pile them up. He failed utterly in using his wealth for God. He had no thought about what he wanted or about what anyone else needed. He was completely self-centered. This man's priorities were upside down. Jesus pointed out in concluding the parable that, although the man considered himself rich, he did not see that he was a pauper toward God.

> Read aloud Luke 12:13-21. Do you think the rich fool had the right to do as he pleased with his money? Why or why not? What did God say to the man in this parable? How could the rich fool have stored up treasures in heaven?

Imagine that each of the following persons are near when the rich fool speaks in Luke 12:17-19. How do you think they would respond to his words? Write or draw about their responses.

A seriously ill child

A homeless person

A poor older adult

Commercials

Think about television commercials. Many seem to say that persons will be more desirable or better people somehow if they buy the advertised products. Think about a familiar commercial. What are the values the commercial expresses? What does it say about our value as human beings? What does it say about the place of possessions in our lives? Write about or draw a familiar commercial below:

It Has Been Said

Read the following quotations. Think about its meaning, and decide whether you agree with it. Write about your reaction to the quotation in the space provided.

Which means most to you? Why? Do the Scriptures in this session support any of the quotations? Which ones? In what ways? Do the Scriptures say anything not covered in the quotations? What?

"Anyone who has more than his necessities possesses the goods of another." (Augustine)

"Gain all you can. . . . Save all you can. . . . Give all you can." (John Wesley)

"If we are to follow a theology of enough, it will mean that in whatever capacity we serve, our lifestyle will be a modest one. . . . By living the lifestyle of enough, we are making a witness to our own faith and challenging the principalities and powers of wealth and security. One who is constantly living at the low end of the range of his or her associates is constantly challenging their lifestyle. If I can operate effectively, living well below the average of my peers, then it would appear that the average is too high." (William Diehl in *Thank God, It's Monday*, Fortress, 1982)

I Say ...

Consider the following open-ended sentences. Based upon the Scriptures and activities in this session, think about the role of possessions in your life and about the messages about possessions that society sends you. How would you complete the sentences?

(1) To be rich means

(2) To seek first God's will means

> Write sentence completions on a chalkboard or a large sheet of paper. Discuss your responses with the entire group. What do these responses say to you about what to do with what your have?

(3) I know I am loved because

(4) If I lost all my possessions today,

(5) If I could rescue only one thing (not a person or a pet) from my burning house, it would be

(6) If I had to take a job at half the salary I make now,

(7) The most important reason for having possessions is

(8) The next important reason for having possessions is

— CLOSING WORSHIP —

Sing again the song "Seek Ye First." Pray together the following prayer:
"Gracious Lord, help each of us to think about what you have graciously given us to possess. We know that what you give is given for your purposes. Guide our living this coming week so we do not hold on to our things but rather use them to your glory; this we pray in Jesus' name. Amen."

Session 10

What Happens When I Pray?

Nancy Regensburger

FOCUS This session will help young adults gain a sense of God's presence and loving concern about their thoughts, longings, relationships, and actions.

— GATHERING —

Greet one another. Find a partner. Tell one another about two or three friends who know you very well. What qualities do those persons bring to your friendships? What do their friendships teach you about your response to others? about your response to God?

Pray together:
"God, you offer us steadfast friendship inside and outside of prayer. Help us find ways to offer our friendship to you as we explore what happens when we pray; in the friendship of Jesus we pray. Amen."

Relationship With God

Any attempt on our part to imagine God is inadequate. God is far more than we can think or visualize. Yet we must imagine God in some way if we are to have any relationship with God.

The Bible is full of meaningful images of God—rock, fire, wind, shield, fountain, fortress. Yet the personal ones are the ones we like best. God is like a mother or a father, a friend, a shepherd, or a spouse. The warmth of these human relationships provides a foundation for understanding our relationship with God.

Communication is the basis of all our relationships. In our friendship with God, we identify conversation as prayer. But in any friendship, communication is not just talking. Communication also involves listening, touching, caressing, writing and reading letters, remembering, and sitting in silence. These forms are also appropriate in our communication with God.

Talking about a growing relationship with God makes little sense if we are not praying. Only through communication do we know we are accepted and experience the power of love. The decision to pray is the decision to offer our friendship to God who already offers friendship to us.

What Is a Friend?

A friend is someone with whom we can be ourselves, someone who loves us no matter how we feel or how we look. If we are tired, we can be silent. If we are distraught, we can rage. If we are in pain, we can cry.

Our prayers should be about what is nearest to our hearts, what is really happening in our lives. Prayer is not only expressing good and holy thoughts or saying things that we think might please God. Instead, prayer is offering ourselves and our thoughts and feelings to God. No concern is too insignificant to discuss with God. We do not need to put on a proper face with someone who knows us as well as God does. Honesty, trust, and commitment are marks of a loving friendship with God as well as with others. Our prayers should reflect our assurance that God loves us as we are.

While God is not a human person, we relate to God in a personal way. Recognizing that the comparison has limits, we can still gain insight by comparing our relationship with others to our relationship with God. Relationships are never static. We might visualize them as cyclical; that is, they circle forward—or backward. Some friendship cycles might be short, such as with a teacher or a mail carrier. Some might last a lifetime, such as marriage and parenting. A human love relationship offers us a way to think about our relationship with God.

Imagine that you have just met someone you like very much and would like to develop a friendship. What are some concrete things you might do to make that come about? List answers below:

Tell the entire group what you listed in order to develop a friendship. What roles do spending time together and communication have in a developing friendships? What do our ideas about ways to develop a friendship teach us about prayer?

Getting to Know You

This dimension of a relationship can involve much talk, gift giving, time together, dating, romance, passion, enthusiasm, falling in love. It is more about, "I need you," and generally cannot be sustained for long periods of time. It is more a doorway to an opportunity for deeper relationship.

A similar doorway emerges in our relationship with God. We may experience enthusiasm, awe, and joy. The good feelings of our religious experiences are important to us. In this phase of relationship with God, we may engage in talk-

What additional words or phrases might describe this dimension of human relationship? When have you or someone you know felt this way about another person? What are some characteristics of communication in this section? What does this dimension of human relationship say to you about relationship with God?

ing prayers—adoration, petition, intercession, and thanksgiving. Read each of the following Scriptures and write any insights you gain from them about prayer and about relationship with God.

The Song of Solomon 3

Hosea 2:14-17

Daniel 4:34-35

Philippians 4:4-7

Disillusionment

Another dimension of human relationship involves disillusionment. A close friend may prefer other friends. A spouse may be
cranky at breakfast. A roommate left the cap off the toothpaste.
Honesty leads to hurt and apologies and more hurt. The relationship may not feel safe. You begin to realize that you are separate
people and that each of you wants things your way. You experience pain, but not a breakup.

Prayer provides the occasion for expressing our disillusionment
to God, and perhaps, with God. We express our fear, frustration,
and anger. We confess our wrongs and apologize. Read the following Scriptures and write about your insights on prayer.

Exodus 17:4

Jeremiah 20:7

Job 7:16-20

James 5:16

> What additional words or phrases might describe this dimension of human relationship? When have you or someone you know felt this way about another person? What are some characteristics of communication in this section? What does this dimension of human relationship say to you about relationship with God?

Parallel Tracks

This dimension of human relationship often feels like walking alone rather than side-by-side. People share less in common. Life and the relationship feel dull and merely functional. People may remain together out of habit. They may be out of touch. Certainly the passion is missing. A positive aspect of this dimension of human relationship is that people can begin to respect differences and to support one another in those differences.

Our relationship with God sometimes takes on this character. It may seem dry or dark. We may experience emptiness, loneliness, and little communication. Oddly, at the same time, we may also find that such times are occasions for growing in our faith and trust. Prayers may be various expressions of "Where are you, God?" Read the following Scriptures and write about any insights they offer you about prayer.

Psalm 13:1-4

Psalm 22:1-2

Psalm 137:1-4

What additional words or phrases might describe this dimension of human relationship? When have you or someone you know felt this way about another person? What are some characteristics of communication in this section? What does this dimension of human relationship say to you about relationship with God?

Isaiah 5:1-7

Isaiah 65:1

Mature Love

The most mature dimension of human relationship involves commitment. Committed relationships may involve much silence. They certainly offer persons a sense of peace, safety, and comfort. Saying "I love you" and "holding hands" involve much more than passion and need; they are expressions of the reality of "we're in it together until the end."

Relationship with God often has such a dimension. Prayers are expressions of peace, joy, adoration, thanksgiving, and praise; and they are occasions for recognizing God's steadfast and faithful presence and love. Meditation and contemplation are silent ways of praying in which we recognize that God is with us. Always. Read the following Scriptures and write about any insights they offer you about prayer.

Hosea 2:16-20

Matthew 26:36-42

Matthew 6:9-10

> What additional words or phrases might describe this dimension of human relationship? When have you or someone you know felt this way about another person? What are some characteristics of communication in this section? What does this dimension of human relationship say to you about relationship with God?

1 Kings 19:11-13a

Psalm 150

Consider Why You Pray

People have many reasons for praying. Many times we relate to others and to God out of need. We all have needs, and nothing is wrong about praying because of a need. But we also know that in relationships based on need, persons can become self-centered, jealous, and grasping. As a healthy relationship develops, we attempt to manipulate the other person less. We move from control to freedom. As we begin to let go, the relationship is motivated less by need and more by love. Look at the following list of reasons for praying. What would you add to the list?

> Which items on the reasons to pray list are primarily prayers of need and which are primarily prayers of love. Put N or L in front of each to indicate which kind of prayer it is. Can some be both?

- difficulty in a relationship
- feeling weak in the face of responsibility
- problems related to raising children

- guidance in making a difficult decision
- telling God about feelings
- asking for forgiveness for wrongdoings
- thanking God for beauty in nature
- asking for help to resist temptation
- expressing love for God
- asking for help during grief or another crisis

Looking at Your Relationship With God

Prayerfully consider where you are in your relationship with God. How would you characterize it at this moment?

Now, write a simple prayer telling God where you are and where you would like to move next in your friendship with God. Your prayer might include examples like these: "God, I don't know you at all, but I would like to know you. Help me take the first step." Or "God, right now I don't even want to learn to pray. It sounds boring. So help me want to pray." Or "I often talk to you a lot, God, but my prayers are selfish. Help me care more about other people and events in the world."

God Speaks First

In our relationship with God we should remember this principle: God does speak, and God always speaks first. How does God speak? We can hear God's Word in Scripture, in nature, through the love of others, in the voice of conscience. God takes the initiative, and we can choose to respond or not to respond. Our desire to pray at all has already been prompted by the Holy Spirit (Romans 8:26).

For all the parallels between our human relationships and our relationship with God, the two are still vastly different. God does not have the imperfections of human friends. God is all faithfulness, patience, perseverance, and love. God alone is truly trustworthy. Our human friendships are between equals; but when we respond to God, we step across the boundary of the natural world into the word of the transcendent. We surpass the limits of what is human and touch what is divine. When that connection happens, it is never because of our own efforts. It is a gift of God.

— CLOSING WORSHIP —

Read aloud Isaiah 65:1:
> "I was ready to be sought out by those who did not ask,
>   to be found by those who did not seek me.
> I said, 'Here I am, here I am,'
>   to a nation that did not call on my name."

Pray silently for a few moments. You may want to pray the prayer you just wrote. Make a commitment to God to offer a word of love—a compliment, appreciation, thanks, encouragement—to another person at least once a day during the coming week. Make a commitment to spend time in prayer each day during the coming week.

Close the session by praying aloud the Lord's Prayer.

Session 11

How Does God Answer Prayer?

Pamela Dilmore

FOCUS This session will help young adults understand how God answers prayer and how their lives reflect those answers.

– GATHERING –

Read aloud Matthew 7:7. Sing the song "Seek Ye First."

Pray aloud the following prayer:
"God of love, sometimes it seems that our prayers are unanswered. Help us through this session to grow in our understanding of the ways you answer our prayers; in Christ, we pray. Amen."

Understanding God and Answered Prayer

The way we understand God and the way we understand prayer are strong influences on the way we understand God's answers to prayer. If we understand God as a sort of Santa Claus provider who responds to our "letters," giving us what we ask for, then we might say our prayer is answered if we get what we ask for. Conversely, we might say our prayer is unanswered if we do not get what we ask for. Most of us at some level can feel the inadequacy of this model of answered prayer. It is a very limited model.

If we understand God as one who longs for our companionship and love and who views prayer as the activity through which we seek that companionship and love, then answered or unanswered prayer might depend on whether or not we experience God's presence.

If we understand God as the one in whom all creation lives, moves, and has its being, we may feel that all prayer is presumptuous. God already knows what we need and provides it.

> How do you understand God? What other ways of understanding God would you add to those listed? What implications would this additional understanding of God have on your understanding of answered prayer?

If we understand God as one who needs our talents and activity for the purposes of love and healing, and if we understand our prayer as seeking God's will, answers to prayer may be our understanding of how to participate in God's loving, healing activity.

Answered prayer embraces all these understandings and others as well. Becoming more open in our desire to hear and see God's answers can be an exciting dimension of our spiritual formation.

Compare Your Prayer

Just how does God answer prayer? Experiences vary. Read the following comparisons and check the ones that best describe your experience with prayer, answered and unanswered.

> Which comparisons did you mark? Why?

___ I put my money in the soda machine, and a drink pops out.

___ I make a phone call, and no one is home.

___ I make a phone call, and the voice mail takes my message.

___ I make a phone call and enjoy a lovely conversation with a friend.

___ I go to the grocery store, and the checkout clerk wants me to pay for what I have picked out.

___ I jump out of an airplane, and my parachute opens.

___ I jump out of an airplane, and my parachute does not open.

___ I fall backwards into a refreshing pool of water on a hot August day.

___ I cast my fishing line, and a brown trout takes my fly.

___ I cast my fishing line, and it gets hung in a tree.

___ I invite a friend to dinner, and we enjoy food and conversation.

___ A friend invites me to dinner, and we enjoy food and conversation.

___ I breathe fresh, clear air and feel cleansed.

___ I breathe fresh clear air and start coughing.

___ I ask a parent for help, and he or she makes me do it myself.

___ A parent asks to help me, and I want to do it myself.

Make a prayer collage. Label one section of a sheet of poster paper "Answered prayer is like ___" and another section "Unanswered prayer is like___." Find pictures in magazines that illustrate the way you would finish these sentences and use the pictures to make a collage by gluing the pictures into the sections near the heading they illustrate. Tell the entire group what your collage means to you.

Write or draw your own prayer comparison in the following space.

Answered prayer:

Unanswered prayer:

Praying Fervently

The story of Peter's escape from jail in Acts 12:1-17 is a vivid description of the way early Christians perceived the activity and power of God. After James was killed and Peter was arrested, the church "prayed fervently" for Peter. When Peter was rescued, he "thought he was seeing a vision" but soon realized the help was real. He escaped, went to Mary's house, and knocked on the door. Rhoda was overjoyed and ran to tell everyone that Peter was at the gate. His friends accused Rhoda of being out of her mind until they saw Peter. Peter described "how the Lord had brought him out of the prison."

What scene was most vivid for you? What character seemed most like where you are now in your life? What did you learn about your own life from the story? What, if anything, did the experience teach you about ways you need to grow in your understanding of how God answers prayer? Did you experience an answer to a prayer in your own life? If so, what? What did God reveal to you from this Scripture?

The story offers opportunities to explore the meaning of hope in desperate times, the community love expressed in "fervent" prayer, and the understanding of life events as God's saving activity. Read the story of Peter's escape from prison and allow your God-given imagination to place yourself in the story in the various roles.

Read Acts 12:1-5. Imagine yourself as Herod, as Peter, as a soldier, as a believer. What do you see? hear? smell? feel? think? What images or situations in your life, if any, does this story make you think about? Pay attention to what you imagine and write any insights or reflections that occur to you:

Read Acts 12:6. Imagine yourself as Peter and as a guard. What do you see? hear? smell? feel? think? What images or situations, if any, emerge from your life? Write about your impressions in the following space.

Read Acts 12:7-11. Place yourself in Peter's position and in the angel's position. What do you see? hear? smell? feel? think? What images or situations, if any, emerge from your life? Write about your impressions below.

Read Acts 12:12-17. Imagine yourself as Peter, as Rhoda, as the other believers. What do you see? hear? smell? feel? think? What images or situations, if any, emerge from your life? Write about your impressions in the following space.

What Do We Really Need?

The Bible challenges us to stretch and risk new ways of under-standing God, prayer, and the ways God answers prayer. Each of the biblical passages in this activity focuses on a different way to understand how God answers prayer. Read each of the following Scriptures and write responses to the questions.

Romans 8:26-27. God searches the heart and discovers what we truly need for wholeness of being. What we need and what we think we need are often not the same. We may think we need a particular person, thing, or event to fill an empty place in our lives when what we really need is much deeper. Our basic human need is to experience and participate in the presence and purposes of God. Humans often try to fill this basic need with material pleasures, personal relationships, success in a career, or any number of other legitimate desires. Yet, fulfilling such desires inevitably falls short of providing deep satisfaction. The Spirit "helps us in our weakness" and "intercedes" when we pray. God's will for the world is salvation-healing, wholeness, justice, and peace. God's will is the activity of love. God searches our hearts and knows what we really need. We can be sure that God's answer to our prayer will be a response that results in our growth toward wholeness and love.

What did you learn from Romans 8:26-27 about ways God answers prayer? What, if anything, challenges you about this Scripture? In what ways does the Scripture challenge you to grow in understanding ways God answers prayer?

Matthew 7:7-11. Jesus says to ask and it will be given, to search and we will find, to knock and it will be opened. These teachings encourage persistence in prayer and making our wants and needs known to God. Jesus uses deeply poetic language to communicate the idea that the God

> Find a partner. Talk about your responses to the Scripture readings. If you have time, share the highlights of your conversation with the entire group.

who loves us will give us what we need. What we need may not be what we specifically request in prayer.

Jesus uses the image of a child making requests. In each case the child asks for what is nourishing, bread and fish. God provides what is needed. Our culture places distorted focus upon self-fulfillment and instant gratification. The child is more likely to ask for candy when the real need is for milk and fresh vegetables.

We are likely to request what "tastes" or "feels" good or what temporarily alleviates our discomfort. God will give us what is ultimately good, nourishes us, and contributes to our spiritual growth.

What did you learn from Matthew 7:7-11 about ways God answers prayer? What, if anything, challenges you about this Scripture? In what ways does the Scripture challenge you to grow in understanding the ways God answers prayer?

Psalm 65. This psalm praises God and recognizes dependence upon the power of God for all life and provision. It lists forgiveness, presence or relationship with humans, deliverance, creation, growth, and the ongoing processes of life as gifts from God. Psalm 65:4 names that which satisfies, the goodness of God's house. Being in God's house is an excellent way to think about being in the presence of God, and being in the presence of God satisfies our deepest needs.

What did you learn from Psalm 65 about ways God answers prayer? What, if anything, challenges you about this Scripture? In what ways does the Scripture challenge you to grow in your understanding of ways God answers prayer?

God Hears Our Prayer

As we have explored in this session, God hears and answers prayer in many ways. How God answers our prayer may not be what we desire or expect. We can be assured, however, that God is always with us, that God hears our prayers, and that God cares for us.

— CLOSING WORSHIP —

Participate in a prayer litany. Write a one-sentence prayer on a small sheet of paper. When everyone has finished, stand in a circle, join hands, and take turns praying your sentence aloud. After someone prays a sentence, other members say, "Thank you, God, for hearing our prayer."
When everyone who wishes to pray has prayed, close with the following prayer:
"God, thank you for teaching us new ways to hear and see your answers to our prayers. Thank you for being with us when we see and when we do not see, when we hear and when we do not hear; in Jesus' love we pray. Amen."

Session 12

Why and How Should I Pray?

Pamela Dilmore

FOCUS This session will help young adults think through their need for a personal prayer life and consider some practical approaches to developing a personal prayer life.

– GATHERING –

Experience silent prayer. Sit in a way that supports your back. Place both feet comfortably on the floor. Place your hands together in front of your heart with only the tips of your fingers slightly touching. Close your eyes, become still, and simply listen to your breathing for a moment. After a few moments of silence, pray the following prayer:

"God, why should I pray? I am not sure what it means to pray. What do I gain from prayer? What do you gain from prayer? Can I really communicate with you? I want to, God. Teach me. Help me. Show me why I need to pray and how I can pray; in the love of Christ. Amen."

What Is Prayer?

Why should I pray? What will prayer do for me? What are the benefits of prayer? Is it really possible to communicate with God? These questions have to do with motivations for prayer, and they emerge from a deeper question. What is prayer? The English word *prayer* comes from the Latin root *precarious*, which has to do with asking or inquiring. The English word *precarious* comes from the same root and describes results that are uncertain. If prayer is simply asking God for something and not knowing whether the something will be given, why pray?

The Greek word used in Matthew 6 for *prayer* is *proseuchomai*, and it means more than asking for specific things. It includes a sense of motion toward, having access to, or being near something. It also means to pray, will, or wish. Prayer, then, means moving toward, having access to, and being near God at the same time we offer our requests, feelings, desires, and will to God. Prayer is our conscious movement into relationship with God.

Look at the word *prayer* that follows. Think of words or phrases that answer the question, What is prayer? These words and phrases should begin with the letters in the word *prayer*. Write these words and phrases near the appropriate letter in the space provided.

P

R

A

Y

E

R

The Center of Prayer

Conscious openness to and movement toward God, whatever form it takes, is prayer; and prayer has many forms. It is silence and sound. It is feeling and thinking. It is stillness and movement. It is action and inaction. It is the aim and the end, the journey and the destination.

At the center of all forms of Christian prayer is the always present Spirit of God, who radiates the energy of new life and love.

Session 12: Why and How Should I Pray?

Prayer forms such as meditation, silence, body prayer, litanies, writing, reading, intercession, adoration, confession, thanksgiving, and supplication, to name a few, are tools to help us relate to God's loving, energizing, healing presence. The person who prays responds to the realities of life, whatever they may be, by moving toward the Reality, toward God.

If prayer is our conscious movement into the presence, power, and love of God, then all life may be lived as prayer. The Scripture passages for this session show a clear interaction between prayer and life. Even

> **How do you experience the presence, power, and love of God?**

when the form of prayer is solitude or being alone with God, it is followed by a renewed immersion into the stream of life. A prayerful life breathes with rhythms of being and doing in the presence of God.

Prayer in all its forms is a spiritual discipline in which we open our hearts and minds to spiritual formation. A disciple is a learner. To learn, a person must see, hear, and practice a skill, behavior, or idea. A spiritual discipline is a regular practice that nourishes our openness to growth in awareness of God's love and will. When we are open, God's Spirit is able to nourish our growth in love. We are "shaped" or "formed" in the ways of peace, justice, and love. Our desire to live in the will of God increases. This kind of growth is spiritual formation.

How can we develop a practice of prayer that nourishes growth in our consciousness of God and our participation in the activities of God? We begin with our intention. We bring who we are with our joys and sorrows, our strengths and weaknesses, our successes and shortcomings to God. The moment we make a conscious movement toward God, who is always present, our prayer has begun.

Belief or Doubt

Look at the following statements about prayer. Think about whether you believe or doubt the statement. Place a mark on the line that indicates what you think or feel about the statement.

1. God will not hear my prayer unless I find a secluded location and pray alone.

I believe it _____I doubt it

2. If I do not get what I pray for, it means I did not pray the right way or I did not have enough faith.

I believe it _____I doubt it

3. God prefers that prayer be done in beautiful, poetic language.

I believe it _____I doubt it

4. I should only pray for others, never just for myself or my needs.

I believe it _____I doubt it

5. Prayer is a sincere opening of my heart and mind to God.

I believe it _____I doubt it

6. God wants me to pray for what I need.

I believe it _____I doubt it

7. It is wrong to pray for my material needs.

I believe it _____I doubt it

8. Since God is in charge of everything, I do not need to pray.

I believe it _____I doubt it

9. To pray means to become more aware of God's presence and love.

I believe it _____I doubt it

Session 12: Why and How Should I Pray?

10. We need to forgive others before we ask God to forgive us.

I believe it _____ I doubt it

What Does Jesus Teach Us About Prayer?

In Matthew 6:5-8, Jesus creates a sharp contrast between the hypocrite who prays publicly to be noticed and the person who prays secretly behind a closed door. The issue is not whether one may be seen praying but rather the motivations for prayer. Private or secret prayer is less likely to be contaminated by external motivations or the need for approval from others. Matthew 6:19-21 addresses these motivations directly by calling attention to eternal values.

Read Matthew 6:5–8, 19–21. This passage asks what we value and what motivates our prayer. In what ways does the passage challenge you? give you strength?

The Lord's Prayer in Matthew 6:9-15 acknowledges the holiness of God and the desire for God's reign and God's will before asking for specific needs. Asking for one's daily bread focuses on what is required for life one day at a time. The prayer for forgiveness depends upon the grace to forgive others. Asking to be rescued from temptation and evil acknowledges our dependence upon the power and grace of God. Read the prayer and think about what it says. In the following space rewrite the prayer in your own words. You may want to read your paraphrased version of the Lord's Prayer aloud to the group.

Mark's Gospel emphasizes the power and authority of God through Jesus the Christ. In Mark 11:20-25, the story of the withered fig tree provides an occasion to teach about faith and belief in God. The dictionary tells us that faith is unquestioning belief, trust, loyalty, confidence, reliance, and allegiance. Jesus taught the disciples they should have faith in God, believe in what they asked for, and not doubt in their hearts. What difficult teachings! Does this mean that if I do not receive what I pray for, I do not have enough faith? Jesus uses belief, faith, and doubt to talk about the quality of one's conscious relationship to God.

The word *faith* is related to words that mean to urge or convince. The Greek word used in Mark is *pistis*, which means "persuasion or conviction." Here the object of faith is God.

> Read Mark 11:22–24. In what ways does this Scripture challenge you? give you strength? How does it illuminate the meaning of the words *faith*, *belief*, and *doubt*? What connections do you see to prayer?

Jesus is saying, in essence, be persuaded of the truthfulness of God. Rely on God. Be true to God who will be true to you. Faith energizes the capacity to choose and act when results are not immediately clear or visible.

What does *believe* mean? The word *believe* is yet another form of the Greek word used for "faith." In Mark's Gospel it means more than simply accepting the truth or reality of a thing; it means to place one's trust in the power and love of God. As with faith, belief has an active, energetic dimension.

Doubt or *diakrino* means more than "second thoughts about the truth of a matter." It also means to separate thoroughly, withdraw from, or oppose. Jesus is saying not to separate or withdraw your heart from God. When one's heart is united with God's, one's prayer is within God's desires or will. One desires what God desires, and such prayers will not be denied.

Luke 6:12-16 tells us that Jesus prayed all night before choosing twelve disciples from among his followers. Prayer is not simply withdrawing from life. Prayer prepares one for the choices and activities of life. It provides resources such as energy, wisdom, guidance, and a sense of God's presence and love. Choosing the Twelve was a critical task for Jesus. Before he chose, he prayed; and his example shines for us. When we make decisions, we must seek the presence, wisdom, and guidance of God.

Session 12: Why and How Should I Pray?

In Luke 18:1-8, Jesus teaches that prayer is an option in dealing with feelings of weakness, weariness, or failure. Such feelings must have been common for a people ruled by the Romans. The Greek word for the phrase "*not to lose heart*" is *ekkakeo,* which means "to be weak, to faint, to fail, or to be weary."

> Read Luke 6:12–16 and 18:1–8. What insights about prayer do these Scriptures offer you?

When life situations cause us to lose hope or want to give up, Jesus says, "Pray." If a judge who respects neither God nor people will attend to the needs of a widow, the God who loves will certainly hear our cries for mercy and justice. Jesus focuses on both justice and persistence in this parable's teaching about prayer.

The Unity of Prayer and Life

Prayer is not simply about the individual. It is intimately related to all of life. First Thessalonians 5:12-22 demonstrates that prayer accompanies loving behavior toward one's neighbor. Paul calls early Christians to rejoice, to pray without ceasing, and to give thanks. Prayer is not an activity divorced from living one's life. It is the matrix from which one's life of love emerges. James 5:13-18 presents the prayer of faith as intercessory prayer, that is, prayer for the needs of others as well as for our own needs. Think about the needs of people you know, the needs of the community or church, and the needs of the world. Write a prayer in the following space.

Who We Are and How We Pray

People are different. It follows that different people pray in different ways. Compare yourself with the people listed below. Who is most like you? Who is most different from you?

Ronna is a very organized person, a planner who appreciates predictability and the security of routines. She reads her Bible every morning and evening. She writes a list of her prayer concerns and joys every day. She prays by talking to God.

Ted is an artist who is intuitive and free-spirited. He loves beauty. He lights candles and incense and looks at a painting of Jesus to help him focus on God.

Marie loves to sing, clap her hands, and attend Christian concerts. She experiences God's presence in her feelings. She raises her hands and sometimes speaks in tongues when she prays.

Which person prays most nearly the way you like to pray? Which prayer form seems most different from yours? Do any of the ways these people pray seem unusual to you? Which ones? In what ways are they unusual ? Do you see a prayer style that you would like to try? Which one? What appeals to you about it?

James loves the outdoors and activities like rappelling and mountain climbing. He often sits on a cliff or a mountaintop to sense God's presence. He likes just being with God.

Suzanne is a receptionist and an outgoing person who loves people. She experiences God's presence through people. She is a member of a group that prays regularly for others. When she is alone, she talks out loud to God.

Hernando is a medical doctor who deeply treasures time when he can be alone. He sits still, becomes silent, and pays attention to his breathing to help him relax in God's presence.

Lee is a student who loves to run and to do stretching exercises. Lee likes to match verses from the Bible with body movement when he prays.

Kristin enjoys traditional worship. She loves to pray the litanies and prayers printed in the order of worship each Sunday. Praying aloud with others in this worship setting makes her feel close to

God and less alone. Sometimes she tapes the order of worship to her refrigerator and reads it during the week.

So, How Do I Pray?

Think about your prayer life. Consider the following questions. Do I have a regular, set-aside time simply to be available to God? When could I allow fifteen to thirty minutes just to be with God? What form of prayer seems most meaningful to me? In what ways could I become more aware of God's presence as I go about the tasks of my day?

The following prayer assignments will give you a taste of several different ways to pray. Pray a different assignment each day for several days. In the space provided, make some notes about your prayer experience.

(1) Choose two or three of your favorite Scripture passages and write your name into the text, making it your text. Example: "Pamela, you shall love the Lord your God with all your heart, and with all your soul, and with all your mind" (Matthew 22:37).

(2) Write the name of a friend or a loved one on a sheet of paper. Be still, close your eyes, and imagine that friend is here with you. Imagine God's love glowing like light all around your friend. Give thanks to God for loving your friend.

(3) Think about the feelings you have had during the week. What are they? joy? sadness? anger? frustration? hope? despair? need? Repeat the following sentence, placing your feeling or feelings in the blank. "God, I give you my _____. Thank you for loving me. Thank you for being here."

(4) Write an ACTS prayer. A is for adoration. Write a sentence of praise or adoration to God. C is for confession. Write a sentence telling God what you need to confess. T is for thanksgiving. Write a sentence expressing thankfulness to God. S is for supplication, or asking. Write a sentence asking God for what you need.

(5) Choose a heart prayer, or unceasing prayer. Ask God to help you think of a simple word, phrase, or Scripture verse. The word might be *love, peace,* or *Jesus.* Or you might choose a simple verse such as "Love one another." Become quiet and relaxed. Repeat the word or phrase over and over. Let the word or phrase match your breathing. Let the word or phrase be your heart prayer.

— CLOSING WORSHIP —

Pray together the following litany:
Leader: Loving God, we can pray in so many ways.

Group: You are with us in whatever way we choose to pray.

Leader: We want to experience you, God, in our hearts, in our minds, in all our being and doing.

Group: When we desire your presence, you are nearer to us than our breath.
[Pray silently for a few moments]

Leader and Group: We thank you, God. We open our lives to your love. We pray as Jesus taught us to pray ... [recite the Lord's Prayer].

Session 13

What Is Christian Commitment?

Nancy Regensburger

FOCUS This session will help young adults look at the nature of discipleship and invite them to experience discipleship for themselves.

– GATHERING –

Greet one another. Find a partner and together, write a definition of the word *commitment*. What does it mean to you? Share your definitions with the entire group.
Pray the following prayer:
"God, help us as we explore Christian commitment. Guide us as we discover the meaning and freedom of commitment to Jesus Christ, in whose name we pray. Amen."

"I Promise ..."

Which commitments do you make to yourself? to values you hold? to others? to God? What is frightening about making commitments? What are the rewards? Why are commitments important?

Commitments are promises or obligations that we make to others. Some are written, some are verbal, and some are simply assumed. Some, such as marriage or parenthood, are lifetime commitments. Others, such as paying a bill or showing up for work, are specific and short-term.

List some of the commitments you now have.

Discipleship

Discipleship, commitment, bearing a cross, servanthood, and self-sacrifice are not popular concepts today. These ideals might not even be honored or practiced in Christian circles, perhaps partly because they have been misunderstood.

When preparing to write on a topic, I frequently run ideas past a good Christian friend to gain insights. Once I asked my friend, "If you were to write about carrying your cross, what would you say?"

I was not prepared for the intensity of her response. "Don't talk to me about bearing crosses. I heard that all through my childhood. My father laid a lot of misery and guilt on Mom and me, and all under the slogan of cross-bearing. So I don't want to hear about crosses!"

> Think of someone you know personally, a public figure, or a historical character who made a great sacrifice for the sake of a commitment. Why do you think the person chose to do this? What do you think was the motive? What was the reward?

No wonder taking up the cross is seen as a depressing experience. Let's be clear: Self-sacrifice does not mean being a doormat and allowing oneself to be trampled. Giving up oneself does not mean neglecting self—our health, education, or spiritual growth. We need to take care of ourselves so we can better serve God and others. Neither is cross-bearing a burden others can force upon us. We freely choose it. On the other hand, others should never use the idea of bearing a cross to hold down persons who are already weak and vulnerable. In those cases, the persons in power need to learn about self-sacrifice.

Remember an occasion when you gave up something for someone else or for a cause. Write responses to the following questions:

What was your motive?

What were the rewards?

What is frightening about making commitments?

To become a disciple of Jesus means a commitment to self-denial and cross-bearing. We freely choose this commitment, based on love for God and for others. When service is motivated by love, it becomes joy rather than drudgery. Love is not a feeling; love is a commitment. When feelings falter, commitment continues until the feelings return, often at a deeper level. Commitment changes the nature of relationship.

Read Matthew 16:24–28. What challenges you about this Scripture? How do you understand Jesus' words, "For those who want to save their life will lose it, and those who lose their life for my sake will find it" (verse 25)?

The Cost of Discipleship

In Matthew 16:24-28, Jesus talks about the cost of discipleship. He says to his disciples, "If any want to become my followers, let them deny themselves and take up their cross and follow me" (Matthew 16:24). He emphasizes true life over selfish interests that have no ultimate value. The word translated "life" in 16:25 in the New Revised Standard Version is translated "soul" or "self" in other translations. The Greek word *psyche* carries all these meanings. "Life," "soul," and "self" are all proper understandings of what is involved in discipleship. To offer one's true self to Christ is to discover life.

Taking up the cross may involve giving up things. But it is even more. As Jesus said, those who want to be his disciples must deny self, take up the cross, and follow him. How can we give up self? The self that Jesus was talking about is not our true self, the one made in the image of God. The self Jesus wants us to give up is the sinful self, the selfish self, the self that says, "I'm Number One." When my selfish self is in control, I think only of *my* fun, *my* clothes, *my* goals, *my* ideas. And when my life is so full of myself, there is no room for others and God.

Identify one selfish part of your life you should give up in order to deny self.

When Jesus said we should take up our cross, he meant that discipleship may bring suffering and even death. Not every Christian will be a martyr, but we are called to be willing to go that far. Service, servanthood, and ministering to others are the focal points of the life of a Christian.

Name something small you could give up for the sake of someone else.

Finally, Jesus said we are to follow him. Jesus' life and sacrificial death are examples for us. He is the total of what we are to do and be. Like Jesus, we are to live a life of love centered on others and on God.

Session 13: What Is Christian Commitment?

Summarize in your own words what you think it means to make a commitment to Jesus.

What Is a Commitment to Discipleship"

The word *disciple* comes from roots that mean "to learn." To be a disciple is to be committed to a teacher or leader in order to learn a way of life. A disciple of Jesus Christ is one who learns the ways of God through Jesus Christ and who makes a commitment to live according to Christ's example and teachings. Look at the word *disciple*. Beside each letter, write a quality of a faithful disciple that begins with that letter.

D

I

S

C

I

P

L

E

Look at what you have written. What insights do you gain about what it means to be a disciple? Use those insights or the ideas they suggest to you to write a poem as follows:

Line 1: Write only *Disciple.*
Line 2: Write two words describing a disciple.
Line 3: Write three action words for a disciple.
Line 4: Write four feeling words about discipleship.
Line 5: Write one word meaning the same as *disciple.*

A Great Treasure

Matthew 13:44 recalls a parable that Jesus told that illustrates the great value of God's kingdom. It uses the image of a treasure. "The kingdom of heaven is like treasure hidden in a field, which someone found and hid; then in his joy he goes and sells all that he has and buys that field."

What do you think Jesus' audience expected the treasure to be? How does our society define *treasure?* What treasure was Jesus talking about? What did the man in the parable give up for the treasure? Why did the man sell everything to get the treasure?

Imagine that you are the one in the parable who has found the treasure. You are alone on a walk in the country. It is a beautiful warm day. The sun is shining. Birds are singing. As you continue your walk, you realize you are in a field. The soil is loose, although still easy to walk on. Suddenly your foot strikes an object in the ground. What can it be? You stoop and brush away the earth. It seems to be the top of a pottery container. You look around. No one is in sight. Rapidly you dig away the soft ground. You tug on the vessel. It sticks. Dig some more. Pull. Finally the earth gives way, and the pottery container is before you. You open it slowly. Suddenly you feel great joy. Within the earthen vessel is a wonderful treasure. What is that treasure for you? Write about the treasure below.

Now you must decide what to do with the treasure. If someone sees you taking it out of the field, you may be accused of stealing. Quickly you place the pottery container back into the ground, cover it over, and sit down in the warm sunshine to think. You decide that if you want to possess the treasure, you will have to buy the field. Then the treasure in the field will be yours. There is no other way. Because you have so little and the field costs so much, you will have to sell everything to buy the field. Is possessing the treasure worth giving up everything? You must make a decision—keep what you now have and miss the treasure, or give up everything and possess the treasure. What do you decide? Write about your decision below.

> What insights did you gain by placing yourself within the parable? What did you identify as the treasure? What did you learn about yourself? about God? about your values? What connections do you make between the parable and commitment? discipleship? God's kingdom?

God Supports Us

As disciples of Jesus Christ, we often falter in our commitments to ourselves, to others, and to God. When we do, God stands ready to forgive. One of the most persistent messages of the Bible is God's faithfulness to us. Commitment, self-sacrifice, servanthood, and bearing our cross define Christian discipleship; and Christian discipleship leads to life, love, and hope. When we are ready to make a commitment to God's way of life as lived and taught through Jesus, we can be assured that God is faithful to us. In spite of our imperfections, we know that nothing will be able to separate us from the love of God in Christ Jesus.

— CLOSING WORSHIP —

Sing together "Are Ye Able." Pray together the following prayer: "God of hope and life, we give you thanks for your constant love through Jesus Christ. Lead us and support us as we commit ourselves to live as his disciples; in Christ we pray. Amen."